CW01513105

Guns Gangs and the implication for social workers

Claudine Duberry

There you the you support you have you Claudine

New Generation Publishing

"Crime is the struggle of isolated individuals, against the prevailing conditions that are dictated by those in power who represent only their own interest", thus criminals "are a by-product of the rich getting richer and the poor getting poorer".

(Roberson, Garrido. 2015, p. 80-81)

I would like to thank Kingston University (social work department) for the inspiration of this book.

In 2007 I undertook the masters in Social work at Kingston University. It came as a surprise that over the years, there had been no considerable reform of the course. The reader may ask how it is possible for the author to voice such an all-encompassing statement. As the author (and past student) I am able to make this audacious statement, because I had been in the social work profession with a great deal of experience and knowledge, for over two decades before undertaking this professional training. My experience of the profession, highlighted that the demand on social workers and the delivery of services had changed over time, in line with the social norms, social deprivation, government policy changes and implementation, and an ever evolving population.

However, the delivery of social work education had not evolved to reflect the needs or demands of the profession. One such area which is lacking in knowledge and exploration, is the growing incidence of violence. Domestic violence, peer violence and what society readily term as "Gang violence". It is believed that this phenomena, is prevalent within society, and a topic of importance in many government departments, however no consideration of its implications are given during the education process. Notwithstanding this, newly qualified social worker, continue to be exposed to the ongoing occurrences of peer violence, and gun and gang violence, without any prior knowledge or understanding of its implications.

If we are guided by the media 'Guns and gangs' are predominantly a black issue. However, although it may be necessary to refer to statistics which directly relate to BME children and young people, there is no colour in this

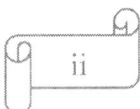

book as the provision of services should not see the colour of a young person's skin, but should be provide dependant on needs.

The intention of this book, is to provide the reader with an understanding of the effects of guns and gangs and its implication for your practice and well-being. The contents will provoke questions which require answers, either in the training environment or during practice. It will equip you with an understanding of the rise of the 'Gangs' and how they are regarded by society. More importantly it will offer you an alternative Perception of victim and perpetrator, who are often children and young people caught up in a cycle which often threatens their very existence.

Further, to this, during your training it is implied that as a service provider you are in the driving seat, as you provide a service that is needed. However, in reality, the mentality of this group is one of self-reliant, thus they neither need nor desire your intervention, and as such they are often challenging, rebellious and in the driving seat, as the only consequence for not engaging with services has been incarceration.

As a reader you can take from this book what informs and empowers you and leave the rest for a later date in time.

I would like to thank my daughter Luwana for her support, and encouraging me to put my experience and knowledge into something tangible.

Thanks to Mr Campbell (aka Uncle Larry) for the constant eye you have on the ball in supporting this book and the provision of the works done by 'Taking Positive Steps' and associates.

To my daughter Natalie, I would like to say thank you for being you.

To my sons I would like to thank them for the experiences we have shared in the criminal justice system.

Mrs Diaz although the sea parts us you were instrumental in keeping me focused, and ensuring that this book got to publication.

I would like to say a special thank you to the 'great grandparents' who wanted their experience to be known but wanted to remain nameless. You have done a fantastic job with you children who are our grandparents and great grandparents to our children, and no societal norms can rob you of that.

To the young people I was and am fortunate enough to work with in the criminal justice system, those who feel they don't have a voice and that they live in a bigoted society, I say thank you for the trust you put in me, thank you for sharing your experiences with me, thank you for making me that confidant you can call on knowing I will think outside the box to help you find a solution. And in all said and done, I say to you "stop and take a look at what you actions are doing to our families, your families and siblings your parents and grandparents and to your children. There are many ways to fight a war and your prevailing actions is not the way.

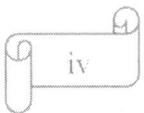

A special thank you to Mr Pusey. Working with you kept me on my toes as well as developing my knowledge of the youth justice system, it taught me how vulnerable young people can be in the youth justice system, and how easy it can be for a young person to lose all hope and become suicidal within the bigoted system.

Claudine Duberry has many years' experience of working with young offenders in the criminal justice system. Working as a remand social worker, Claudine was able to identify the difficulties faced by young people in court, the courts' system, the prison system and the youth justice board. Claudine was influential in setting up one of the first Independent Advisory Groups (IAG) in London (Hackney) which was a recommendation of the McPherson report in 1999, and for some time worked alongside Trident. In undertaking voluntary works with the community, which is inclusive of the longest siege in the UK (Hackney) Claudine has been awarded a number of commendations by the MPS. Claudine Duberry, is the founding Director of Taking Positive Steps and Associates Ltd (TPS). Claudine is a motivational speaker, consultant, and a mentor. TPS provides cost effective, comprehensive, personalised consultancy and training to professionals who work and engage with young people who are on the periphery or involved in crime. In addition to this TPS provides a tailored resettlement service to young people ostracised and excluded from society.

"Murders of children by other children have tripled in over the years, as more of the nation's youth get drawn into a deadly world of guns and knives" (Wynne-Jones and Leapman, 2008)

There is an assumption that young people in the past where well mannered, disciplined, law abiding and somewhat different from today's youth. However, Dumfries, (1994: 21) (cited at "London Gangs" 2008) disputed this position, acknowledging that there is nothing new about gangs and street violence, and in reality juvenile crime is deeply rooted in our past. Regardless of whether gangs and guns are historic or a new phenomenon recently a series of tragic and high-profile shootings has raised the issue of gang and gang membership in both the public consciousness and the political arena. With a background of bonnet youngsters posing with guns being aired in the media, there have been renewed calls to crack down on the activities of these youngsters and to prevent them from becoming involved in gang violence.

As noted public concern regarding violent youth crime is at an unprecedented high, as demonstrated by figures published by the Youth Justice Board (telegraph.co.uk). At the time of writing this paper I was concerned about the unsystematic approach that is often persuasively referred to as gang violence. I felt there was a need to better understand what was really happening on our streets with and with our youth, who are often propelled into a life of violence, criminality, hopelessness and despair. It may or may not be agreed that the delinquent behaviour displayed by Britain's gangs are the product of various pathways, often found in the most deprived and marginalised communities suffering high family breakdown, various addiction (drugs and or alcohol) and unemployment.

The impact of guns, gangs, delinquent behaviour and the increases in youth crime stories and frustrated parents

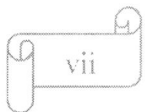

seeking help for their troubled children, has put policies' relating to Juvenile justice at the centre of public attention and political debate in recent years. Furthermore, the increasingly violent nature of present-day youth crime, and the escalating number of young people involved with the juvenile justice system have challenged established beliefs guiding government policies and professional practice within various sectors.

There are various professions-services (health, police, court, etc.) who come into contact with youth and gun crime, and as such it is asked can social services (workers) play a role in preventing gang crime and its involvement? In an attempt to answer this question, Batmanghelidjh of Kids Company (Community Care Live online) says, "social services lack capacity to tackle gang involvement". She further contended "Children's social services have no capacity to use child protection measures to support young people at risk of gang involvement". Batmanghelidjh, whose organisation worked with highly vulnerable young people,(until 2015) made the comments in relation to calls from Metropolitan Police Commissioner Sir Ian Blair for a "child protection approach" to support siblings of young people involved in gangs (Community Care Live online).

The rise of the "Gangs" in London

To the reader,

This document (The rise of the "Gangs" in London) is for your information and only seeks to provide you with a background history to the rise of the gangs in London, and some of the "Gangs" of London. There is no part of this document which has been produced or re-produced by "Tacking Positive Steps Ltd" and we take no responsibility for the information contained herein.

Vanessa (Freelists.org, 2014) wrote, in the late 1970's, a group of individuals known as the Broadwater Farm Posse were active on the Broadwater Farm estate (see Broadwater Farm Posse). The Tottenham Mandem, known originally as 'Frontliners' or 'Totten'am Boys', were a follow on generation to the Farm Posse who had firmly established their reputation by the time of the 1985 riots on the Broadwater Farm estate. Police Constable Keith Blakelock was murdered during the course of those riots. When alleged Broadwater Farm Posse member Winston Silcott was first in custody after the riots, during questioning after being asked did you murder Police Constable Blakelock, the police claimed he had been put in the frame by local youths, also with alleged involvement.

Amongst those kids allegedly involved was Mark Lambie. Lambie was born in 1971 and acquired a string of violent offences as a youth. As said, his first major allegation was the murder of PC Blakelock, who was

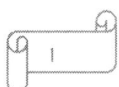

1

hacked to death, in 1985 when he was just 14. Lambie laughed as the case against him and two other juveniles collapsed.

In the following years he built up a fearsome reputation for shootings, robbery, kidnap, torture and drug-running. Flaunting gold jewellery, designer clothes and expensive cars, he went on the lead the Tottenham Mandem gang after the older generation had moved away from the gritty end of the business, staying in the background to organise and arrange drugs and firearms for the street gangsters of north London. Lambie's first major conviction was in 1991 following a gang shooting in Holloway to which he pleaded guilty for assault occasioning actual bodily harm. By the mid-1990's, Lambie had links across London (in other notorious areas such as Harlesden, Ladbroke Grove, Lambeth and Lewisham) and beyond.

He and the Tottenham Mandem took control over large parts of London's street drug trade, often by force and extreme violence. By 1995, one of his main rivals was another alleged street gangster Jerome Maddix. There was a drive-by at Maddix's home and he was murdered the following year in Jamaica. Maddix's murder was followed by a series of tit-for-tat shootings between TMD and their rivals from northwest London. Lambie was believed to be an associate of the Lock City Crew, who were also engaged in rivalry with another northwest London 'Yardie' gang. Several murders had occurred by the late 1990's involving older criminals linked to Tottenham and Harlesden, one of which saw disc jockey Laverne Forbes and her partner Patrick 'Nookie' Smith gunned down at their home on the Ferry Lane estate N17.

In 1996, police believed that Lambie and an associate Clifford Angol were behind the shooting and wounding of Kenneth Rowe in Willesden. Rowe, originally from Stamford Hill, had been part of a gang of steamers from South Tottenham, Stamford Hill and Clapton, called the DMC Posse in the late 1980's. Rowe declined to aid police in his shooting. The following April, in what appeared to be an attack against Lambie, two men were shot in a case of mistaken identity at the Place To Be Caribbean restaurant in Kensal Rise. Three gunmen walked into the restaurant asking for 'Mark' to identify himself. Mark Lambie, who was believed to have been there, kept quiet. Instead two other men identified themselves and taking no precautions the gunmen shot both. One was Mark Spence, an unemployed painter and decorator, who was immediately shot dead. The other, Mark Verley, was shot in the spine and paralysed. He died sometime later.

It is not known whether or not Kenneth Rowe was one of the gunmen but six weeks later he himself was shot dead in Mount Pleasant Lane, Upper Clapton. Lambie and Angol, suspects in the earlier shooting, were arrested although there was insufficient evidence. A couple of days later Clifford Angol was shot dead as he sat in Lambie's BMW outside the Warwick Castle Pub in Portobello Road. The gunman had pulled up beside him in a yellow car and calmly shot him six times.

The youngest generation of Tottenham Mandem began to establish their fearsome and violent reputation from 1996-97. The TMD sphere of control in north London at that point was tremendous. They had influence over a host of new developing gangs that also arose in the late 1990's such as Edmonton Firm, Wood Green Firm, Hornsey, parts of N19 and bits of N16. This younger generation grew in secondary schools amongst young teens from 1994-95, together they were the 'Firm' encompassing the aforementioned areas, but they started to become independent by 1996-97. The wider gang organisation grew to become seemingly a very organised unit of bosses, lieutenants, soldiers and areas based groups.

The older generations were responsible for different parts of north London and the local drug markets. At the top was Mark Lambie, known also as "The Prince of Darkness" or as "Phantom". He was the boss of the 'street team' that was TMD. Above him remained the old timers who maintained drug and firearm connections amongst the organised criminal element with links to the Caribbean. Below Lambie there was lieutenants who controlled geographical areas: these included men such as Anthony Bourne, known as Blue from Edmonton, who headed the Edmonton Firm (sometimes referred to as Edmonton Mandem), Warren Leader was based in Wood Green and then there was a host of infamous Tottenham criminals. In 1997, the youngers of TMD, aged predominantly in their mid to late teens, came into conflict with another gang predominantly from London Fields in Hackney. It was one of London's most bloodiest and intense gang rivalries claiming several lives in six years.

Tottenham Mandem versus Hackney Boys (London Fields) 1997-2003 At this point in time the Hackney Boys. were predominantly from the London Fields area although were close to other Hackney Boys on the Pembury and Mothers Square estates, it was not quite a borough wide gang but covered the E2/E5/E8 postcodes. According to the book, Guns and Gangs, by Grahame McLagan the police Operation Trident unit put the start of the war down to the killing of Guydance Dacres, 16, who was shot dead in Chimes in January 1997. It occurred at a private party when Tottenham Mandem associate Anthony 'Blue' Bourne was alleged to have fired a gun at the club which hit and killed Hackney youth Dacres. However, the real ignition is believed by many to have been brought on earlier. In 1995, a couple of youths from Tottenham had been friendly with youths from London Fields and Pembury, they went out together robbing people, including young dealers, in other parts of north London. They also went on steaming robberies across shops. The Tottenham youths however started to come back to Hackney and re-rob the Hackney youths which caused very serious grievances. One of the TMD youths stabbed a Hackney Boy from Pembury in the leg during one of the re-robberies, an act which led to a series of cyclical violence between the two areas. Rare Tottenham & Hackney Link Up - The Slums Im From. A couple of TMD youths were confronted by Hackney Boys follwing this, which incidentally also came a month after the murder of Dacres. The TMD boys were chased but one youth, Kingsley 'Popcorn' Iyasara was cornered into a block of flats on the Carlton Lodge estate, a small estate around Carlton Road just north of Finsbury Park. He was beaten up and then shot dead in the presence of at least six members of the Hackney Boys. He bled to death on the roof of a block of flats. The 16-year-old Popcorn was well known and well connected in the Tottenham area. One TMD youth, and later music artist Clint Ponton, helped convict the six suspects from Hackney having also been chased along with Popcorn, and whilst a single killer was not identified the suspects were all sentenced at the Old Bailey for between four and six years each. It was also alleged Ponton had arranged a deal with the seventh suspect who was found not guilty. The Hackney youths were largely from London Fields, whilst TMD where largely from Broadwater Farm. Although this conflict is often labelled Hackney versus

Tottenham, it's really more linked to those two estates within each borough. The series of killings and reprisals between the two areas really kicked off in the late 1990's. Two of those convicted for the murder of Popcorn were shot dead by TMD soon after their release from prison in separate incidents. In June 1999, Meneliek Robinson, 20, was driving his red BMW convertible in Hackney when it was followed by two motorbikes. One pulled in front of the BMW, blocking its way, whilst another stopped beside it. The pillion passenger dismounted and walked up to the side window firing several shots. Two years later in April 2001 another of the Hackney Boys convicted, Corey Wright, 20, was also shot dead in his car in Hackney. His friend who was with him, Wayne Henry, was also killed. The shots fired into Wright's BMW caused the vehicle to lose control and it went off the road into a bus stop by Thistlethwaite Road in Lower Clapton. These were some of the 8 gang and organised crime related killings that earned Lower and Upper Clapton Road the reputation as 'Murder Mile'.

Although the murders were never solved, some people believe Clint Ponton had some involvement and it is alleged he contacted the Hackney Boys to deny his involvement a couple of days after the murders of Wright and Henry. Hackney responded with the murder of TMD / Firm member Adrian 'Buckhead' Crawford from Edmonton. He was murdered in December 2002 after being shot down in a hail of bullets in front of his pregnant girlfriend in West Green Road, Tottenham. Hackney Boy Daniel 'DC' Cummings, who was also a Hounslow club promoter, was pinned with the murder having been identified by witnesses. However, Clint Ponton again comes into the frame according to street legends. They go along the lines that Daniel Cummings was not behind the killing but Clint Ponton had forced Crawford's girlfriend to identify Cummings, a strategic move of sorts.

Cummings has been serving a life sentence since 2003. A series of events following the Crawford murder led to the eventual death of Hackney boy Jason Fearon. It happened at Turnmills club in Clerkenwell during a So Solid Crew event (an act managed by Tottenham Mandem's later NorthStar team) where singer Lisa Maffia was to be promoting her debut single. An anonymous tip-off was made to Crimestoppers that there would be trouble at the event and there was an attempt to prevent the event going ahead but the event organiser refused. As a result the police parked a vehicle outside the club hoping that would deter any would be gunmen.

However, in the early hours several men burst into the nightclub firing shots, injuring one person. The gunfire continued as the targets were chased into the street. Jason Fearon and another man, who police believe was the main target, made away in an Audi TT sports car. They were followed by two Tottenham men, who police believed to be Clint Ponton and Wes Lambie, firing shots into the Audi from their BMW during a car chase. Fearon who was

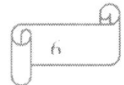

wearing a bullet proof vest was hit in the head and died. Clint Ponton, also known as C1 or The Chosen One, and Wes Lambie went into the music industry forming the label NorthStar whilst with the Tottenham Mandem.

Meanwhile, in the background to these seven killings, Mark Lambie had become a target of the recently formed Metropolitan Police unit Operation Trident. Bringing Down Lambie By 2000, Lambie had gained a reputation for being untouchable and for having mythical powers, believed by some to possess 'ju-ju powers' - of being a Obeahman, a Jamaican voodoo spirit who can never be killed. He become the number one nominal for Operation Trident detectives. Despite his high ranking position he was still involved in shooting incidents. In November 1999, he was named as the shooter in an incident at the Coliseum nightclub in Vauxhaul, south London. He was charged with attempted murder but the victim later withdrew the evidence, as many victims of TMD and their predecessors have always done. In another incident, Lambie and a man known as Michael 'Mallet' Thomas, fired shots at the EQ nightclub in Hackney. After this incident, Stephan Grant was shot dead, believed to be by TMD members. Six firearms were found in an abandoned car at the scene.

In another drug related shooting in 2000, Hackney dealer Darren Henry was shot dead in Sandal Road, Upper Edmonton N18. He had been lured to the area by rival drug dealer Andrew Martin who had kidnapped Henry's half brothers and held them hostage. He shot Henry between the shoulder blades with a handgun before leading police on a high speed chase. Kidnapping rivals from Hackney was a trait of Lambie and Tottenham, but it would be his downfall. Police suspected Lambie in many cases but never had enough evidence to stick. It was not until the 19th April 2001 that they caught him 'at it'.

The day started with police following Lambie from his Streatham home to Tottenham where he met up with friends and associates. Things began to look interesting for officers when they all moved off together in a convoy of three vehicles with the police following. However, they come across difficulties fairly quickly as the cars drove into the Broadwater Farm estate, police decided it was too risky to follow because they were mostly white and would have stood out on the predominantly black estate. Instead they waited outside the estate hoping to see Lambie drive off. He was seen leaving in a Golf together with a blue sports car. After a few minutes the sports car was abandoned and the driver got into Lambie's car. The two then drove to south Tottenham and parked up in Turner Avenue before attending a house party on a nearby estate. There had been 12-hours surveillance and it looked as though nothing was going to happen and the detectives decided they were going to call it a day. On getting back to Tottenham police station a Jamaican, frightened and injured, dashed into the station with an amazing story of kidnap and torture by Lambie. It emerged that it had happened right under the noses of the surveillance team as they were sitting waiting outside Broadwater Farm. Jamaican Gregory 'Beenie Man' Smith and his friend Towayne 'Tupac' Morris had been lured to the estate by Lambie's associate Anthony 'Blue' Bourne who said they wanted to meet to discuss a mutual girlfriend. The Jamaicans headed there in the blue sports car detectives had seen abandoned earlier that day. They told detectives how they had been pistol whipped and bundled into the boots of two cars and taken to an address near Turner Avenue. They were taken to the upstairs room of a flat and attacked and tortured with a hammer and kettle of hot water whilst threatened to pay £20,000 in drugs and cash to Lambie. Smith had managed to escape and ran to the police station. Mark Lambie and Anthony Bourne were convicted of kidnap and blackmail and sentenced to 12-years in May 2002. Other gang members Warren Leader and Francis Osei were also convicted. Lambie and Bourne have finished serving their sentences for these offences. Clint Ponton was cleared of all charges and freed.

Even after Lambie's arrest, Trident killings continued to occur around the Farm and across Tottenham Mandem's area. In October 2001, an 18-year-old, Tyrone Rowe, was shot dead as he and his friends were in a car on West Green Road near the Ida estate on route to a party. A second man was discovered near the scene with stomach wounds. The killer was described as a black man, aged around 30 and wearing a three-quarter length black leather jacket. No motive has ever been established and the case remains unsolved. In 2010 an appeal was made urging those with information to come forward and help end the families' ordeal.

A £10,000 reward is being offered for information leading to a prosecution. Shortly after the killing, three men were spotted driving a lime green people carrier towards Wood Green.

In June 2002, Harrington Mark Jack, 31, also known by various other names including Andrew Brown or by first names Douglas and Doug, was shot dead at a flat in Ermine House, Moselle Street by White Hart Lane. Known by the street name 'Dog', he was shot during a scuffle with two men which could have been witnessed by a dozen people. A young man was then stabbed to death on the Chestnut estate in October 2002. Less than a year later, in March 2003, 41-year-old Patrick Anthony Morrison from Edmonton was shot dead in the stairwell of a housing block on Broadwater Farm. All killings remain unsolved. CCTV cameras on the Broadwater Farm estate captured the events around the killing of 28-year-old Gavin Smith in October 2003. He was dragged from his car into a block of flats before being taken to Lordship Recreation Ground where he was found dead. This was one attributed by the police to the Yardies. Jason McDonald and Dwayne Millwood were accused of inflicting the fatal stab wounds.

Jamaican Millwood blamed the killing on another gangster who was deported.

Smith came to London from Jamaica in 2000 and lived in Lewisham, he was involved in drug dealing, delivering and collecting packages on behalf of the boyfriend of his sister, Donald Vincent. He fell foul of rivals whilst making a call at Tangmere House on the Farm. In March 2004, TMD member Marcus Cox was shot dead on Tottenham High Road. He was gunned down by a fearful Syron Martin.

The killing was shown on an episode of TV documentary 'Murder Blues', which followed cases of Operation Trident in London, see below links.

NorthStar

NorthStar was the creation of long term TMD member Clint Ponton. It began in 2003 as a result of their links with urban music group 'So Solid Crew' through Megaman and Lambie. After Ponton had escaped being tried for the murder of Jason Fearon, he created NorthStar as a legitimate music front / enterprise, following on from the days of TMD. NorthStar had links with numerous other music crews that had been closely linked to older gangs such as Poverty Driven Children in Brixton. They also maintained historical links that Mark Lambie gained with areas such as Harlesden / Kensal Green and the Ghetto Boys. in south London.   Whilst members maintain that NorthStar is for entertainment purposes only and sourcing local music talent, the name is the influence for 'Star Gang' (see BWF FMD.). C1 / Clint Ponton - Northstar Freestyle 2005.

The hatred between Broadwater Farm and London Fields still exists to this day. As for those involved in the war between 1997-2003, their rivalries have continued to play out through music. Songs disrespecting one another have been produced, including one whereby NorthStar refer to their rivals as 'Trashtown' (a manipulation of London Fields music group 'Mash Town').   Whilst this conflict rarely erupts in violence, it is merely just dormant rather than over. In February 2009, Clint Ponton and Wes Lambie, younger brother to Mark Lambie, were assaulted at the Urban Music Awards, hosted at the O2 arena. Ponton was stabbed with a champagne bottle during the attack, which was alleged retaliation for a shooting in 2008 that targeted a younger brother of a former Hackney Boy, Corey Wright. Often failing to stay out of the limelight for the wrong reasons, in 2010 Ponton was at the Tottenham Carnival where his younger brother had his chain snatched by members of the Young Dem Africans gang from Edmonton. Another case involving members of the TMD in recent years was that of Gary Guthrie who was gunned down in the street. The men arrested were all long time members of the Tottenham Mandem and Poverty Driven Children. Jamaican Guthrie died from a single gunshot wound to the chest on Steatham High Road in the early hours of the morning on Monday 22nd October 2007. Poverty Driven Children individuals Courtney Hutchinson, Nathan 'Inch' Cross and Darrell 'Bumbles' Albert, alongside Tottenham Mandem individuals Junior 'Killa Cam' Cameron, Michael 'Tall Mike' Wabara and Simon 'Redz' Rhodes-Butler were tried at the Old Bailey. The victim and his friend Rowan Williams were confronted after leaving an event at the Starlight Rooms. Although no motive has ever been established, there is evidence that there was a shared intention on the basis that a number of defendants were armed with loaded firearms. The victims, both Jamaican, arrived at the club by 2am, whilst the defendants, described by witnesses as 'English boys', arrived after 4am. They were different from the Jamaican crowd, dressing more casually and forming their own group within the club, which by the time of their arrival was winding down.

The club closed at 5am and CCTV captured Guthrie leaving with Rowan. It showed Hutchinson and Cole deliberately moving in front of them. A convoy of vehicles stopped shortly after alongside Guthrie and Rowan's vehicle, and following an argument, the pair were shot at by two men with loaded guns. Junior Cameron was said to have fired the fatal shot with a Steyr self-loading pistol whilst Darrell Albert is said to have shot Williams using a Baikal IZH-79 9mm pistol.

The Steyr pistol was found behind a bath panel at Cameron's home in Enfield following his arrest in January 2008. Cameron had a long criminal history, beginning at the age of 13. He came from a broken home, both his parents were addicted to drugs, and he lived with his grandmother until she died when he was just seven at which point he was taken into care. He had previous convictions for possession of firearms and knives, burglary and robbery. In 2005 he was jailed for perverting the course of justice after setting fire to the car that belonged to murdered Turkish drug dealer Oguzhan Ozdemir who was shot dead after being abducted in 2001. An officer in the trial claimed Cameron was a habitual carrier of guns who had threatened to use a gun against the officer. Cameron denied the claim, telling court that this particular officer, PC Jason Eatock, had a reputation for being aggressive with young black boys in Haringey.

PC Eatock from Haringey, alongside another officer, was subject to an IPCC investigation in 2003. for unnecessary force in Haringey. He was also one of three officers involved in a mini-riot in Tottenham's Northumberland Park area in 2010. that began after officers tried to arrest a teenager who had allegedly thrown a knife onto a garage.

With regards to the Guthrie trial, all except Cameron and Albert walked free from court after the judge ruled there was insufficient evidence against them. Cameron was found guilty of Guthrie's murder for having harboured the weapon. After the verdicts were announced Cameron said 'How are they sure? Why don't someone ask how they are sure? They cannot be sure'.

Sets & Cliques

After the Hackney Boys and Tottenham Mandem 'gang-war' period died down many gangs in London began to break down into smaller geographically based sets or cliques. Hackney was probably the first borough to fully develop this trend, hence the high number of gangs currently present in the borough. In Tottenham, the new sets developed across over a dozen housing estates and council residential blocks in N15 and N17 from 2003 onwards. Some of the more prominent of them came to be known as:

Farm Mandem/BWF. Ida Boys. NPK. (Northumberland Park) Tiverton Mandem. Stonebridge (Ermine & Plevna) Other geographical areas of activity are Appleby Close, Bourne & Twyford Hoses, Broad Lane, Chestnut. Grove, Culvert Road, Edgecot Grove, Ferry Lane, Pembury Road (High Road), Reed Road, Saltram Close, Scotland Green, Suffolk Road and White Hart Lane / Bruce Castle.

Any of the above areas today may refer to themselves as Tottenham Mandem (TMD)
    - this is an appreciation of the local area and an acronym that continues to be used by younger members collectively referring to their status as 'Tottenham Mandem'. However, TMD does not really refer to a gang anymore. During the course of larger gangs breaking down, former alliances with neighbouring areas Edmonton (N9) and Wood Green are no more. The relationships between north London gangs have become very contentious amongst the following generations of youths, new rivalries and alliances have been built at more micro-levels that have made the world of gangs in London very crowded. Even within Tottenham there have been internal rivalries that flare up between the new sets and cliques wanting to assert their dominance (Freelists.org, 2014).

Introduction:

It was once the case, that organised criminals used firearms specifically and temporarily to address a given incident or conflict. This was evident in the days of the Kray brothers, when on March 8th, 1966 three men were shot and wounded and one man killed (Greco, 2014). However, although the days of the Krays, sits firmly in the past what is very much in the present is young people who are often armed and dangerous with guns and knives. Disputes which were settled with fists are now settled with knives and handguns. Over the years the succession of youth killings in the UK has astonished, horrified and saddened the nation. The full impact of gang crime in London, was revealed in 2014 with Met figures showing, 6,600 violent offences were committed by gang members in just three years (Evening Standard, 2014). Notwithstanding this, it is equally alarming that children as young as 10 years old in Glasgow, and 11 years old in London were affiliated to a gang.

Many blame the occurrence of youth crime, fundamentally on social issues, which was, corroborated by the Joseph Rowntree Foundation. In 1996 The Joseph Rowntree Foundation, (1996) argued, that there were major risk factors that may predispose youth, to criminal activities. Amongst these risks are, low income and poor housing -low school attainment - poor parental supervision, parental conflict and broken families. Back then these issues were disturbing, however, nineteen years later, the risk factors experienced by youth who were involved in guns, gangs and anti-social behaviour remains the same thus exposing future generations to the same fate. It is acknowledged that with the incidence of guns, gangs and delinquent behaviour becoming more bourgeoning, it may have an impact on the profession of social work and the services provided. However, before looking at the impact of guns, gangs and the implication for social work it is necessary to understand the prevalence, the theories and causes.

Amongst communities, there seems to be a consensus, that the rise of delinquent behaviour, amongst our youth has become a problem, not only in their neighbourhood, but in society as a whole. It is further agreed, that in the past young people were well mannered, disciplined, law abiding and somewhat different in many ways from the youth of today, *where* presentation and behaviour has rapidly changed. In addition to the previously mentioned, concerns the rise of gun and knife crime committed by juvenile gangs remain justified. As this book goes to publication the homicide figures between 2005 and June 2015 stood at 175 (Citizensreportuk.org, n.d.) It cannot be disputed that the UK has seen a rise in gang crime and the use of firearms, albeit to a lesser degree than the United States. This inference was authenticated by the Sydney-based Institute for Economics and Peace (qtd at Hutton, 2013) who verified that the U.K. had 933 violent crimes per 100,000 people in 2012, down from 1,255 in 2003. However, in the U.S., the figure for 2010 was 399 violent crimes per 100,000 people. This report further acknowledged that, whilst the U.S. violent-crime rate is less than half of Britain's, its homicide rate between 2003 and 2011 was almost four times as high (Hutton, 2013) Further to this, findings provided by Hutton, (2013) paves the way for a better understanding of the rise and prevalence of crime, which can be traced back at least twenty years. It is further suggested that these occurrences can be in direct correlation to the Changes in the global economy, particularly the financial market, which has affected both countries with the result been an increase in social exclusion and its associated problems.

There have been various literature written on this growing phenomenon, of gangs, which I shall refer to later whilst looking at the prevalence of this behaviour. However much of the literature and research has been conducted in American, which may have contributed to the tendency, to view gangs as an American phenomenon, a position that was verified at Family.jrank.org.

Whilst the trend of guns and gangs is of growing concern, and somewhat alarming, the problem is far from unique to Britain, emerging worldwide within our communities' and societies, where disaffected and marginalised young people have come together to form groups, who behave in an unsocial way, we term them as 'gangs'. In addition to the rise of the 'new gangs', in 2002 it was suggested that the UK had seen the arrival of young black men coming from Jamaica who they termed as Yardies. It was believed by the media, that the Yardies were Jamaican gangsters who brought with them the ability to command respect albeit with violence, and moved into a lifestyle which was far from the one that they had left behind (Silverman, 1999) Contra to the aforementioned, Journalist Tony Thompson, who researched the Yardie underworld thoroughly in 1995 for his book Gangland Britain, concluded that while Yardies definitely exist, their influence has been blown out of proportion. (BBC News 1999). Irrespective of this what cannot be argued is that before their arrival in the UK many Jamaican men had experienced an impoverished existence, thus it was easy for them to relate to British born young men with the same experience, recruiting them into what became known as, the bling-bling life style. Consequently, in order to live this lifestyle successfully, they, like the young Jamaican men before them believed they needed to command respect from their peers, rival groups and the wider community. This led to them possessing guns. Although a correlation between these groups, is evident to see it is still debatable as to "why this group believe they are unable to reach the standard of living they require-deserve, through legal means? A reasonable response may highlight, the incidence of deprivation, education, socialisation, criminalisation, marketability and access to professional careers as significant factors.

There is no repudiating the fact that youth gangs pose a considerable problem to contemporary society; a realisation which is corroborated by the government, who have invested £4m from 2011-2013 in an attempt to tackle the anti-social behaviour and crime. While the government has ploughed a substantial amount of money into addressing the issues of youth crime, research into why young people engage in gang activity and the lack of departure from such has been scarce, suggesting that further research into the topic is necessary in order to prevent and deter young people from engaging in gang activity.

For many years literature on gangs was sparse within the UK relying on research conducted in America, which highlights that many youth gangs who share some characteristics of the American gangs, have been reported as a growing concern across many countries inclusive of the UK (Family.jrank.org, 2015). However, this position is in conflict with a report produced by the Jill Dando Institute of Crime Science where it argues that there is little evidence to suggest there are many US style gangs in the UK (Marshal, et al, 2005)

Notwithstanding this position, Social Science Collection records (online), highlights that "more than 70 youngsters died at the hands of gangs in Britain in 2008". This research also note, that more than 170 gangs exist in London alone, with members as young as ten years old. Since the publication of the Social science collection findings, the numbers of gangs in the UK have risen to 225 with fifty-eight believed to be active. What is more in 2009 Slack, (2009) highlighted that "Gun crime had almost doubled since Labour came to power, and a culture of dangerous gang violence has taken hold". Further to this, Government figures showed that the total number of firearm offences in England and Wales had increased from 5,209 in 1998/99 to 9,865 in 2008 - a rise of 89 per cent.

Further to this, gang violence showed no signs of subsiding, and in some parts of the country, the number of offences had increased more than five-fold. These published statistic would further fuel fears that the police were struggling to contain gang-related violence, in which the possession of firearms had become increasingly common place.

It was further noted that as youth crime runs out of control, the Government struggles to get a firm grip on it, and as a result an increasing number of children are joining gangs and falling into a life of drugs. Slacks (20090 further revealed, there had been a "six fold increase in the number of gangs in some parts of London since 2000", as well as numbers increasing in the Home Counties. In addition to the above-mentioned, in 2007 it was suspected that a quarter of all gun crimes were committed by youth under-18 years. This theory was evidenced after the killing of 11 years old, Rhys Jones. Rhys was killed, by 16 year old Sean Mercer, and the headlines read "Youth gangs triple child murder rate" (Wynne-Jones and Leapman, (2008) corroborating public perception about the youth-on-youth violence, and the incidence of gang crime. In addition, to an already insufferable situation, came the postcode war. With the rise of the postcode war, youths from the opposite side of the streets were killing each other, and youths have been killed for going into the "wrong" postcode area (Malone, 2009).

If we are to believe the media and relevant publications, it raises the question of who are these gangs and how did they come about?

Many say that the world is getting smaller. This can be verified in the fact that, communication is a lot simpler with the development of technology and we share each other's cultures and life experiences through travel and the importation and exportation of goods. As a result we are living in a huge global economy, where if something happens in one part of the world it can have a rippling effects worldwide. This process is referred to as globalisation. This was validated by Giddens (1990:64, qtd in (Durham and Kellner, 2001, Smith and Doyle, 2013) who argued that "globalisation can be described as the intensification of worldwide social relations, which link distant localities in such a way, that local happenings are shaped by events occurring many miles away" This proclamation, can be evidenced by occurrences of the early 1970's, which saw a decline in the manufacturing industry which affected major inner cities, both in the UK and in the USA. During this period cities such as Chicago, Philadelphia and New York lost more than fifty percent of their manufacturing industry. It may also be accepted that the impact of this decline had a detrimental effect on subordinate communities, consequently permitting the social divisions and income inequality between the rich and the poor during the latter part of the twentieth century to become steadily wider. Additionally, it is thought that these occurrences resulted in greater social problems in the inner cities, an increased poverty and petty crime (Wilson, 1996). As a result thereof, it may be argued that, the delinquent behaviour exhibited by some young people, is a reaction to the fact that their progression, in a capitalist consumer society is not easily attainable.

This is a situation which was experienced by many of their relatives, and community members before them. Moreover, it is not unreasonable to suppose that in areas where high unemployment exists in conjunction with other social disadvantages, people might turn to crime as a way of basic survival.

In looking at the manifestation of gun and gangs and the implication for social work, it is necessary to understand the institution of gangs and how we got here.

Although the prevalence of gangs may cause some alarm and concern, an examination of history informs us that, the presence of gangs and gangsters in the UK is nothing new- and existed long before the notorious Kray brothers. "Peaky Blinders" a drama series featured on BBC (2014) tells the story of one such gang that operated in Birmingham, England's second city, a hundred or so years ago. The Peaky Blinders made money from illegal bookmaking, protection rackets, the underground economy and robbery (Clark 2013). This gang was followed through history by the notorious Kray twins- Ronald and Reginald Kray led a criminal gang that ruled the East End of London by fear between 1950s and 60s. Other gangs such as The Thompson Family, who had a grasp on Glasgow during the 1950s, and the Noonan brothers who were based in Manchester during late 80s, and early 90's also ruled by fear (Edwards, 2012). It may be the case that the presence and reporting of gang crime had declined between the late 70's and early 80's, however they had not disappeared-and with the rising of the new age gangs 'what remains consistent is their ability to create fear and anxiety

Gun's, gangs and knife's seem to be an endemic culture amongst black British youth, where did it originate from and does inequality play a role?

During a House of Commons debates (June 2009), Chris Grayling argued " the truth is those who join gangs often come from the most difficult family backgrounds—from an environment where they feel neglected and unwanted" (they work for you 2009). Within the same debate it was further argued that if we mapped out the geographically rates of unemployment, family breakdown, educational failure and addiction within the family, we would uncover a high correlation linking social breakdown and gang culture. Acceptance of this statement, would serve to remove any misconception of the relationship between deprivation, gang membership and knife crime. Further to this, research by the Sutton Trust has confirmed there is a correlation between certain types of violent crime and inequality (cited at, they work for you.com). In harmony with the preceding position, many described poverty as been a 'trap' constraining peoples' lives and limiting their aspirations (Herald Scotland, n.d.). Furthermore, poverty is also seen as a trigger for other social evils especially those classed as deviant behaviour by youths. Deviant behaviour is any behaviour that is sufficient in its severity to violate social norm which receives disapproval from society. However, it must be acknowledged that deviant behaviour can be criminal or non-criminal, and for the purposes of this book I will only be dealing with those incidences of youth crime (10 and 18 year old) and its impact on society.

Definition of Gangs and who are they.

Gangs and gang behaviour has become a general debate. However, when asked to describe a "gang" and its characteristic, most people would struggle to give an agreed definition on what constitutes a gang. In spite of this, the beginning of this book gave us a history of the "new" gangs of London. This book refers to them as the "New" gangs because as we have seen gangs are not a new phenomenon, but are deep rooted in our history.

As noted above there is no collectively agreed term for gangs. Nevertheless in establishing a definition, of who should be referred to as a gang, it can be asked, Should a group of young men, standing under a street light on a dark winter's night, wearing hoodie's pulled far down over their heads, displaying boisterous behaviour be classed as, or referred to as a gang? In order to answer this question it is important to know what constitutes a "gang". Atkinson and Ubiribo (n/d) further argued that there is no universally accepted definition of a gang, and as such the debate surrounding what is a "gang" has been ongoing for decades. It was further agreed by Clark, (2006) on behalf of the Royal Canadian Mounted Police that "there is no single standard operational definition of Youth gangs". He further maintains, there is a lack of a widely agreed-upon definition within academic, research, government and law enforcement. Clark (2006) further argues that a lack of universally agreed definition hinders the formation of a local, regional and or national database.

This view was agreed by the National Institute of Justice, who also acknowledged "there is no universally agreed-upon definition of "gang" in the United States, nor an agreed definition in the UK. Nevertheless what is evident is, "Gangs, youth gangs and street gangs are

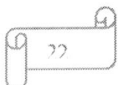

terms widely and often interchangeably used in mainstream coverage".

Traditionally, gangs have been subjected to a plethora of different characterisations, which are dependent upon who is formulating the definition and for what purpose it is been formulated. This viewpoint has contributed to the lack of a universal definition on 'Gangs'. Although there may not be an agreed definition of gangs, Curry and Spergel (1988, qtd at Yearwood and Hayes, 2000) maintains that "gangs are complexly organized, sometimes cohesive and often have established leaders and rules. It was further argued that these groups engage in a wide variety of violent crime, conflict with other gangs and often demonstrate a tradition of possessing distinctive territory, or turf, colours and hand signs" and a gang name. In addition to the above, it is argued that the police's definition of a gang is "a group of individuals, juvenile and or adult, who associate on a continuous basis, form an allegiance for a common purpose, and are involved in delinquent or criminal activity". (Gangout.com, Encyclopedia.com, 2003)

Furthermore, it was argued by Atkinson and Ubiribo, (n.d.) that "the image portrayed by the media is one of organised groups of violent offenders (mostly Black Afro Caribbean Descent) brandishing guns, dealing drugs and constantly involved in bloody inter-gang conflicts" who are not expected to live beyond 24. The presumption of the media was accepted by Tony Blair (Labour Prime minister 1997-2007) who claimed that "the spate of knife and gun murders in London was not being caused by poverty, but a distinctive black culture" (Wintour and Dodd 2007). This representation was far removed from the opinion of Home Office minister Lady Scotland, who told the home affairs select committee "the disproportionate number of black youths in the criminal justice system was a function of their disproportionate poverty, and not to do with a distinctive black culture". She further went on to say "We accept there is an increasing problem with the use of guns, and we are trying to address it". However, we have not had any evidence that this issue is solely or disproportionately an issue for black young men.", (Steele, 2007)

The occurrences of youth gang, and the carrying of weapons, namely knives and guns has been the subject of media and political attention in the UK and other countries for many years. An unpublished report by the Metropolitan police (BBC News, 2007) found that African-Caribbean gangs were described as the largest group, followed by south Asian and white gangs. Despite these findings, and the spotlight given to them, there is considerable misunderstanding about how youth 'gangs' are constituted, what being in or associated with a youth 'gang' means or how their activities may link to other aspects of their everyday lives and experiences. Furthermore, while the term youth 'gang' is entrenched in current political and media dialogue, it remains the case that in order to constructively use the term 'gang', there needs to be a clear classification of whom this refers to, and thus far this seems to be far removed, Clark, (2006). Irrespective of the disagreement of Clark (2006) and others and based on the above mentioned statement by Tony Blair, can we surmise that youths who associate together, are of the same culture, and may commit some crime together is a valid description of a 'gang'

During February 2007 a report by the Metropolitan Police identified 169 gangs (BBC News 2007). This number is significantly higher, at the time this book went to publication. According to current MPS intelligence there are 225 recognised gangs in London, consisting of around 3,600 gang members. Fifty-eight gangs are considered active - accounting for two thirds of offences where a named gang has been identified as being involved (Police, 2015). It is suggested that 'Gangs' range from organised criminal networks involved in Class A drugs' supply and firearms, to street-based gangs involved in violence and personal robbery. This opinion was further brandished by a Metropolitan Police report that highlighted Gangs as "relatively durable, predominantly street based group of people who see themselves (and are seen by others) as a discernible group for whom crime and violence is integral to the group identity" (Metropolitan Police London Gang Profile 2006). However, what is interesting, is the very fact that the young people who are affiliated with these youth groups, do not describe themselves as gangs, but are inclined to refer to themselves as a "crew", a family and the "man dem" amongst others terms, consequently this adds to the ambiguous definition of what characterises a gang.

Accordingly, without a clear definition of what constitutes a gang the Youth Justice Board suggest that by labelling groups of youths involved in petty crime as gangs, risks pushing them towards a life of crime. (BBC Magazine 2007) The Youth Justice Board may have had a valid point in so far as if you authenticate something, you are acknowledging it, thus encouraging a self-fulfilling prophecy (negative beliefs predict negative behaviour) which seems to have come to fruition.

It cannot be argued that these young people have formed affiliations with friends from the same area and post code, and like many before them (Cray brothers) often have, what is socially referred to as turf wars going on between them which has been detrimental to their peers and some innocent bystanders. As noted above, due to the bling culture, the demand of respect

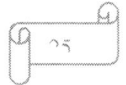

and the turf wars, these young people began by carry knives, which has now been substituted for guns, in order to protect themselves and what they class as their turf-area. These young people are very passionate about their turf, consequently the price for straying into another area (defined as the wrong area or not your manor) could result in robbery, and even the loss of life. It has not been unheard of, for a straying youth to be beaten-up stabbed or shot, this position was confirmed by (Malone, 2009) this seems a high price to pay, for what can be deemed by an outsider as a mistake. Nonetheless, it is a code which is very well known by youths from various post codes who will often voice the fact "they can't travel across borough or even into a neighbouring post code" where turf wars and gang domination were and are still present. This complexity is often misunderstood by professionals, for example, social workers and the benefit agencies. Consequently, young people will often refuse to sign-on at the job centre, police station bail and often have to make alternative arrangements to meet probation officers.

Further, to their ongoing issue with turf wars, and post code, there are also issues about gang rivalry and reprisal attacks. Pitts (2008 p3) notes that in 2003, young black people under the age of 20 constituted 16 per cent of victims of gun crime investigated by Operation Trident. Operation Trident, is the specialist unit, within the Metropolitan Police department responsible for investigating black-on-black crime. Furthermore, by 2006 this number had risen substantially to 31 per cent.

Metropolitan Police (BBC London, 2007) further testified that gangs are responsible for more than a fifth of youth crime in London, with nearly half of the London gangs having been involved in serious assault.

In support of Tony Blair's statement (as above mentioned) the "Police hold black men responsible for more than two-thirds of shootings and more than half of robberies and street crimes in London", this was according to figures released by Scotland Yard in 2010 (Camber, 2010). In further confirmation of this, a police figure for the Met Police proclaimed that "the majority of violent inner-city crime is committed by black men". The statement further went on to acknowledge, statistics also show, black men are twice as likely to be victims of such crimes (Camber, 2010).

Pitt (2008 p4) highlighted that "in London during 2007, 28 young people under the age of 20 were killed in gang-related murders".

In attestation of the aforesaid, figures generated by the Metropolitan Police and the Home Office between April and November 2007, highlighted that 1,273 young people were injured in gun and knife attacks, with the seriousness been broken down in the following way: 321 young people shot (39 serious), 955 were stabbed (188 seriously). Furthermore, It was also reported that the largest number of gangs involved in extortion, drug dealing, robbery and dealing stolen or counterfeit goods are said to be in Hackney, east London (22 gangs); Enfield in north London (13); Lambeth and Merton in south London (12 gangs each); Waltham Forest in north east London (11) and Brent in North West London (11) (BBC News 2007).

With a brief understanding of who is "questionably" labelled as gang members, what some issues are (turf wars, rivalry and revenge) which can contribute to the incidence of gun, knife crime and the conflict it can cause amongst young people, it begs the question of, what make gang life more attractive, than the social norms that society demands, and why would they sign up to it?

Weapons

In the past a survey conducted by the Youth Justice Board (Youth Justice Board 2007, p5) showed that while young people may carry weapons, the weapon of choice was more likely to be a knife and not a gun. They also noted that the majority of young people excluded from mainstream education had carried knives. However, to what extent this trend was customary amongst the said group is not evident. Research published, (Youth Justice Board 2007) noted that "currently there was no national data on knives to support the growing concern about the extent to which knives were carried by young people 10 – 17 years old". Accordingly, as earlier noted it is accepted that there is no uniformed agreement on who gang members are, nor any national data to support societies concerns on the possession of knives by young people. Although the YJB concluded that there was no national data on knives to support the growing concern, a Survey conducted by the market research group MORI, provided information on knife carrying amongst school children in England and Wales from 1999 to 2005. During this survey it was recorded that "in 2005, 5,463 pupils aged 11 to 16 years old were questioned, accordingly it was revealed that 32 per cent of the children and young people surveys, said they had carried a knife in the last 12 months"(Eades et al., 2007). However it is suggested that although a significant number of children and young people admitted to having carried a knife, it does not necessarily correlate to 'knife crime'. This suggestion is supported by, Eades, et al. (2007) who also alluded to the fact that been in possession of a knife is not a conclusive link to 'knife crime'. During the national knife amnesty of 2006, the Metropolitan Police Service released a statement, which informed the public '52 teenagers are victims of knife crime EVERY week in London'. This statement had the ability generate anxiety and distress in communities that were already fragile. Eades, et al. (2007) questioned, "what does 'knife crime' indicated in that sentence"? They further argued that "it is easy to surmise from such a statement that each of those 52 incidents of 'knife crime' involves a stabbing. However, it needs to be remembered, 'knife crime' will not automatically result in a victim who has been physically harmed, even if significant distress is caused. Although the possession of a knife does not equal a victim or a crime, during 2006, the National Youth Agency noted that gun and knife crime had increased dramatically over the previous years. They further noted that incidences of robberies in which a bladed article (knife) was used increased by approximately 15,000 cases and the incidence of firearm offences had increased by 30% in the last two years (Stutz, 2006 P1). It was further argued that these incidences (knives and guns) were and are predominantly an urban problem taking place in the major cities inclusive of London, Manchester and Liverpool (Stutz, 2006 P1). The incidence of guns, gangs and violent behaviour displayed amongst some youth in our society have caused public concern and often moral panic. However, is this concern or moral panic warranted? Sociology expert Ashley Grossman, (2015) described Moral panic as an 'extreme social response, to the belief that the moral condition of society is deteriorating at a rapid pace'. In addition, she highlighted that numerous sociologists, have interpreted moral panic, as a device used to distract public attention, from underlying social problems, and justify increased social control, over the working class and other potentially rebellious segments of society, for example those young people displaying rebellious behaviour. It is the case that public and moral panic often occurs during times when society is unable to adapt to significant change-s, consequently provoking fear, that control within the 'normal' social structure is threatened. Nevertheless and in spite of the publicity and alarm at the spate of murders, guns and knife crime, amongst the inner city teenagers in recent years and months, Britain is not, and has never been in a "state of anarchy" (Times online

2006). Irrespective of the fact that Britain isn't and has never been in a state of anarchy, we are never short of sensational headlines which create an impression of lawlessness and disorder and a repaid disintegration of social norms. Within the social order, as it presently stands, it is regarded as typical for the media to dramatise news, which relates to, and involves gangs of youths. It can be intensely argued, that the media often sensationalise crime, with the intention of generating moral panic. It can be argued, that irrespective of the opinions held by the nation and politicians, the incidence of social and moral panic, is mainly influence by way youth crime is interpreted and reported by the media. Furthermore the strategies used by the media will often motivate the public to come to their own conclusion, and make sense of the events that occur, which ostensibly threaten societal values or social structure. Further, to this, it is also commonplace, for the media to declare, that the incidence of youth crime is out of control, and that something should be done by the government, to facilitate a change. One such incidence which had the ability of generating social panic was the British gun control laws which seemingly didn't go far enough to protect social norms and values pre the Hungerford massacre. The Hungerford Massacre and the Firearms (Amendment) Act 1988 was passed after the Hungerford massacre of 1987, and focussed on the prohibition of semi-automatic shotguns and rifles, the banning of armour piercing ammunition, and tightening controls on shotguns, (AOAV, 2014). In 1996 it revolvers and semi-automatic pistols remained legal with a firearms licence, as were single-shot shotguns and rifles. However moral concerns were once again intensified following the Dunblane massacre in Scotland, where a number of school children and their teacher was shot dead by a lone gunman. This incident, generated national panic and concern for the safety of children in schools and public places. This incident engendered national fare, and led to public and governmental discussions about gun control, and the violent nature of society. These decisions resulted in extensive amendments to gun laws (Firearms Amendment) (No. 2) Act 1997, thus making the United Kingdom one of the strictest countries regarding public access to handguns. However, although Britain has strict gun law policies, the prevalence of guns and fatalities still remain in our communities, thus generating, regular, unfavourable headlines. Williams (2004) argues that in recent years reporting of news bears no resemblance to reporting of the past. Williams (2004 p74) notes that in 1945 incidents were not so graphically reported, however, by the 1970's crimes were increasingly presented as a menace, which are threatening to society. Moreover, by 1989 reporting by the media had developed even further, not only were they reporting full details of the crime, but also pictures identifying the victim and the crime scene. As a result of their actions, not only were the media instigating moral panic, they were also instrumental in governmental policies on law and order, which did not necessarily serve the purpose for which they were intended, or the persons for whom they were intended. This can be further demonstrated if we look at a law which was found in the fines unit of the Criminal Justice Act 1991. Under this Act, the magistrates' court could impose fines up to £5000 for most offences excluding murder and treason. The Crime, Justice and Protecting the Public White Paper, announced a desire to make fines proportionate to the offenders' ability to pay, in order to reduce the number of prisoners serving time for non-payment. The levels of the units introduced by the 1991 Act were: Level 1 - £200, Level 2 - £500, Level 3 - £1000, Level 4 £2500, and Level 5 - £5000; on summary conviction. (Richinstyle.com, 2012) The system did not work, and resulted in absurdly high fines for trivial offences. The Criminal Justice Act 1993 (section 65(1)) restored judicial preference by adding that courts have the power to alter fines according to offenders' means and ability to pay. (Richinstyle.com, 2012) Parents were also made responsible for their children's fines. The maximum fine imposable on a child was-is £250 on summary conviction for an either way offence, or £1000 for a young person on summary conviction for an either way offence. In addition, The Criminal Justice Act 1991, a White Paper published in February 1990 (Home Office, 1990), the Government expressed its intention to enforce parents' responsibility for the criminal acts of their children aged10 and 16 years. Arthur, (2005 p. 2) highlighted that the government wanted to make it a criminal offence for parents to 'fail to prevent their children from committing offences". However, the specified proposal was heavily criticised by many, inclusive of the Magistrates' Association, and was subsequently dropped. Notwithstanding this, the 1991 Act (under the fines unit) was criticised as inappropriate, as most of the young offenders came from families that were already lacking in quality or resources, and had a tendency to live chaotic lifestyles. Consequently if fines were enforced it likely to cause even more poverty and deprivation.

Arthur, (2005 p. 2) confirmed this position as he argued that "most young offenders' lives are characterised by economic and social deprivation, family breakdown and a lack of a positive role model such as an appropriate father figure". It was further contested that the "proposal was likely to be counter-productive in that it might lead to the complete disintegration of already fragile family units" (West, 1982, p. 52; Hall and Martin, 1990, p. 604 qtd in Arthur, 2005 p. 2).

Although there has been various legislation aimed at youth and gang crime, at present there is no law within the UK barring gangs or gang membership, consequently there is no legal deterrent to being a gang member. Regardless of the fact that these young people are not breaking a law by forming a youth gang or socialising together the activities which are associated with their can be lawless. In order to curtail concerning activities, the criminal justice system has seen the introduction of laws and legislation, pertaining to the behaviour and control of young offender's e.g. anti-social behaviour orders and dispersal orders to name a few. Irrespective of such, the incidence of youth association and youth crimes have continued to escalate.

Why do some young people join gangs and become violent offenders?

For a number of years the author worked with young people in what society now term as 'gangs', and the youth justice system and as a result was able to solicit individual perspective as to why young people get involved in anti-social youth behaviour, more commonly referred to as 'gang' crime. What became evident, was there is no answer that fits all, but are inclusive of the following:

> ➢ Some young people are growing up in neighbourhoods where gang life has become a way of life and the norm.

> ➢ Some young people are tired of being picked on by others and want a support system e.g. someone to "have their back"

> ➢ Some young people are looking for respect and power and being part of a gang can command that respect.

This information was confirmed by experts who suggested that young people join gangs because they act as surrogate families, as well as providing a sense of belonging, power, control and prestige; all things that are commonly identified as absent in childhood among gang' (Muller Ph.D., 2013). More often than not, juveniles and those most vulnerable to gang life come from broken homes, many never having had a solid sense of internal belonging and safety. Further, to this some young people have genuine problem at home, which encourages them to turn to what they class as 'street life', where they receive the care and attention that being part of a gang can provide. For these reasons gangs are often seen as a surrogate family. By the same token, others young people want to make money and have designer goods and are in search of instant gratification. The mentality of these young people are often motivated by the media, and their desire to have a better standard of life than the one they often have.

In an attempt to address the aforementioned behaviours, researchers carried out a long-term study around violence in Chicago neighbourhoods, considering why some youth become violent and use guns. By analysing collected data it was recorded that young people who witness gun violence are more likely to engage in violent crime. (Schaffer, 2004) Moreover, it is believed that "youth who live in dangerous, disadvantaged neighbourhoods and have been exposed to violence are more likely to carry guns" (National institutes of Justice 2007). This then begs the question of, has the incidence of poverty, broken homes and witnessed-experienced violence played a role in the development, of this unlawful behaviour we have seen amongst some youth? Decker and Van Winkle (1996) argued that joining a gang consist of both pulls and pushers (Ojjdp.gov, 2008). Within this publication, it is explained that the pulls pertain to the attractiveness of the gangs, for example, gang membership can improve kudos amongst friends along with the opportunity to make money, which they may never have the opportunity to make legitimately (Howell 1998 p. 5). Further, to this it was acknowledged that social, economic and cultural forces have pushed many adolescents in the direction of gangs. It has also been established by some researchers, that the under classed, and marginal minority status experienced by some youth, also serves as a pusher (Wilson 1987). It may then justifiably be argued that these experiences have served to create social disorder.

Social disorganisation theory

In looking at deviant behaviour, criminologists and other social scientists have looked at many components, when trying to elucidate what causes criminal behaviour. In so doing, sociologists have developed several social structure theories in an effort to link criminal behaviour patterns to socio-economic forces and other social environmental factors, one of which is social disorganization theory. Although social disorganisation theory has a long and distinguished history, starting with Park and Burgess (1924), Thrasher (1927) and Shaw and McKay (1942). The rise of psychological approaches for understanding criminal behaviour, led to a declining interest in social disorganisation until the late 20th Century Bursik, (1988). William J. Wilson's (1987) are widely credited for reviving our interest in understanding the influence of this theory (Sutherland et al. 2013 p. 3). Social disorganization theory "argues that crime occurs when the mechanisms of social control (arrest and court procedure, jail sentences and payment of money for breaking the law) are weakened" (Kelly, 2000; Messier, Baud). Further, to this it is a major assumption of social disorganization theory, that crime is caused by social factors or bad places rather than bad people, consequently another term for this perspective is "environmental determinism." However, within this framework, as we are viewing it, social disorganization is defined as "the inability of local communities to realize common values of their residents, or solve commonly experienced problems" (Shaw & McKay, 1942, qtd in O'Connor, 2006, p13, enotes 2014). Additionally research discussed by enotes (2014) highlighted that, "in an attempt to explain why these communities faced social disorganization to such a level, enabling criminal traditions to become embedded, three reasons were given:

- ➢ Residential instability/mobility,
- ➢ Racial-ethnic heterogeneity
- ➢ Poverty:

However Sampson and Groves (1989) argued that if residential instability is uses as an example, this should not be regarded as a direct cause of crime, but as something which 'fosters institutional disruption, and weakened social controls' (Sampson et al., 1997: 919) (Sutherland et al. 2013 p. 3). Likewise, it is through that a lack of contact and the loss of trust in neighbours may contribute to criminal behaviour (Sampson et al, 2005). 'Family disruption' (lone parents) was added to the list by Sampson (1987). Family disruption was thought to affect the ability of parents to manage their own children as well as their capacity to provide guardianship of the local community (Sutherland et al. 2013 p.3).

Sociological perspective on deviant behaviour/guns and gangs

The sociological discipline that deals with crime (behaviour that violates our laws) is known as criminology. The concept of deviance is complex because norms vary considerably across groups, times, and places and countries. In other words, what one group or country may consider acceptable, another may consider deviant such as robbery, theft, rape, murder, and assault, just to name a few. However, as stated earlier, the clarification and attitudes towards antisocial behaviour will be dependent on the group, time and culture. Very recently we have seen the rise of 'group behaviour' the media has termed as gang rape amongst certain groups. However, these young people term it as a 'link', where young women are encouraged by their peers to behave in a way, which is socially unacceptable within the UK. (Channel 4 Dispatches). However sex with a minor or the sharing of a female amongst friends may be acceptable in other cultures or nations. As noted above there are a number of theories relating to deviance and criminology which have emerged over the years. One of the earliest theorists of criminal behaviour was Cesare Lombroso, who believed that criminal behaviour was a result of a person's physical characteristics (Middens, 2001). Cesare Lambroso was a famous positivist criminologist. The primary idea behind positivist criminology is that criminals are born as such, it is the nature of the person, not nurture that results in criminal propensities. (Schubert, 2013)

Since then various criminologists and sociologists have tried to determine the causes of crime. One such theorist was Bowlby (1946) who linked behaviour to parenting. Bowlby argued that, if a child's early needs and nurturing are not met by its mother, and if a close and loving relationship is not established during the early years, then a psychopathic personality is liable to develop. However other theorists have criticised Bowlby's work for a number of reasons, one such reason was that psychoanalytic theories are difficult to assess because they rely on how a person's mind might work.

Additionally in the early days of the theory, academic psychologists criticised Bowlby, and the psychoanalytic community ostracised him for his departure from psychoanalytical tenets (Rutter 1995)

Further to this Bowlby's attachment theory was criticised by J. R. Harris. Harris believed that "if a child is brought up in a crime-ridden area, they will be susceptible to committing these same kinds of crimes. Harris believed that this was due to the "high rate of peer pressure and the want to fit in to the group". Consequently even if parents try to bring up their children the best way they know how, chances are if they associate with delinquents, they will become involved in delinquent behaviour. Further to this Harris argued that if you moved the residential location of a child who is headed down the wrong road, to a new environment such as a small suburban town, there is a chance he will get himself on the right track, because he is trying to fit in with a new peer group (Harris, 1998 qtd in Lee, 2015).

Nevertheless, attachment theory has become the leading approach to understanding early social development, and has given rise to a great surge of empirical investigations into the development of children's close relationships (Schaffer R, 2003). The rise of social constructionism and the popularity of symbolic interactionism led to the notion of labelling. Labelling theory is one of the most important approaches to understanding deviant and criminal behaviour. It stems from the work of W.I. Thomas who, in 1928, wrote, "If men define situations as real, they are real in their consequences" (Grossman, 2015). Grossman (2015) further highlighted that labelling theory is based on the premise that "no act is intrinsically criminal, accordingly the classifications of criminality are established by those in power, through the conceptualisation of laws, and the interpretation and acceptance of those laws by the police, courts, and prison institutes.

Therefore, in understanding the nature of deviance itself, we it is important to first understand why certain people are tagged with a deviant label and others are not. It should be understood that those who represent the judicial system and those who enforce, social norms [behaviours], such as the police, court officials, and school authorities, are responsible for the main source of labelling. In addition to this, many of the rulings that define deviance, and the contexts in which deviant behaviour is labelled as deviant, are framed by the wealthy designed for the poor, by men for women, by older people for younger people etc. The consequences of such is that, the more powerful and prevailing groups in society, make and attach deviant labels to the subordinate groups. Labelling theory has had a great influence on the study of crime and its causation. It has allowed for the re-examine of views on crime and criminals. However, labelling theory is not without its faults and has been criticised. One of the criticisms, argues that labelling theory emphasise the interactive process of labelling and ignores the processes that lead to the deviant acts. Such processes might include differences in socialisation, attitudes, and opportunities. (Roberson, Azaola, 2015, p. 73) Further concerns were raised by Conflict and critical Theory. 'Conflict Theory' a theory promoted by Karl Marx claimed that society is in a state of continuous conflict due to the ongoing competition for limited resources. (Roberson, Azaola, 2015, p. 74) Conflict theory holds that social order is maintained by domination and power, rather than consensus and conformity. According to conflict theory, those with wealth and power try to hold on to it by any means possible, predominantly by suppressing the poor and powerless. Conflict theory also attributes most of the fundamental expansions in human history, such as democracy and civil rights, to capitalistic endeavours to control the masses rather than to a desire for social order. (Investopedia, 2013)

Max did not discuss crime causation and its relationship to the economic system at any length, however what he did argue was that "crime is the struggle of isolated individuals, against the prevailing conditions that are dictated by those in power who represent only their own interest, (Roberson, Azaola, 2015, p. 80-81) thus they are a by-product of the rich getting richer and the poor getting poorer". Those who are a by-product of the deprivation suffered in society may see this division as criminal behaviour which requires further investigation.

Criminological Theory

Criminological research includes the incidence of crime as well as its causes and consequences. Criminology is related to the study of deviant behaviour- those actions which society says departs from social norms, values and beliefs.

Within the UK you may be charged with possessing an illegal substance if you're caught with drugs, whether they're yours or not. The use of Marijuana may be deemed as illegal by law, however can it be classed as deviant behaviour? This is a valid question especially as a substantial amount of the population are either using recreational drugs or have used them in the pass. As a result of this, it can be argued that our system would be seriously flawed to label all behaviours which depart from social norms as criminal. In 2012 Labour's rising star Chuka Umunna confessed to smoking marijuana when he was a teenager. (Walker, 2012)

Criminology the positivist school has attempted to find scientific objectivity for the measurement and quantification of criminal behaviour". The Positivist School of thought presumes that criminal behaviour is caused by various internal and external factors which are outside of the individual's control. The scientific process was introduced and applied to the study of human behaviour. Positivism can be broken up into three segments which include biological, psychological and social positivism. Nation master.com (2013)

From a criminological perspective criminologists would agree that many of society's laws are not neutral, but reflects and protects established economic, racial, and political power and privileged (Siegel, 2000). Whilst Marxists recognise that for a society to function efficiently, social order is necessary, "the founders of Marxism thought that crime, same as all other problems of human society, is a direct result of the unjust structure of capitalism" (Marxism and Criminology). Furthermore, Marx argued that one should always ask of the law who benefits from it? And in doing so, one may note that most laws are formulated to protect the interests of the most powerful members in society from those with the least power (Chambliss, et al.). Siegel, (2000) further argued that crime is a political concept design to protect the power and position of the upper class at the expense of the poor. It may further be argued that crime prevention strategies are, designed in such a way that they uphold societies established notions of social order, consequently working against those who deviate from the given norms for example young people involved in gangs and antisocial behaviour. Irrespective of the aforesaid, it may be argued that there are some law's which are for the greater good and these can include the law against rape, armed robbery, and murder. However Siegel, (2000) argues that the prohibition of these acts are aimed at domestic tranquillity ensuring that the anger of the poor and marginalised classes will not be directed at their wealthy capitalist exploiters.

Notwithstanding the above, a concrete answer to why people become involved in crime still evades society. Furthermore it is the case that when looking at the incidence of crime most criminological theories focus on what makes people "criminal". They look for causes, such as child-rearing practices, genetic make-up, and psychosomatic or social processes. However, these theories are very difficult to test; and are of varying and unknown scientific validity. (Popcenter.org, 2015) Accordingly in view of Siegel's arguments as outlined above it may be necessary to ask is this prevalent point still fundamental or relevant?

On the contrary to the abovementioned, it is the case that the theories and concepts of environmental criminology remain very helpful in everyday police work, and can be equally useful in social work in the deterrent of youth crime. If you are familiar with the process, you will be a stronger member of the problem-oriented team. The problem analysis triangle (also known as the crime triangle) comes from one of the main theories of environmental criminology - routine activity theory. This theory, originally formulated by Lawrence Cohen and Marcus Felsonn, states that "predatory crime occurs when a likely offender and suitable target come together". This theory argues that offenders will make choices based on their perceptions of opportunities. Understanding how offenders see things is an important part of the work that will be undertaken by social workers, as well as the prevention of crime, because almost all crime prevention involves challenging and changing offenders' perceptions of crime (Ronald V. Clarke et al. 2015), criminal opportunities and instant gratification.

Differential-association theory

Edwin Sutherland coined the phrase differential association in order to address the issue of how people learn deviance. Differential-association theory has contributed to the field of criminology in its focus on the developmental nature of criminality. Sutherland, unlike Lombroso believed that the environment plays a major role in deciding which norms people learn to violate. Sutherland aimed to show that people also learn their norms from various socializing agents—parents, teachers, ministers, family, friends, co-workers, and the media. In short, people learn criminal behaviour, like other behaviours, from their interactions with others, especially in intimate groups, hence there is a lot to be said for appropriate socialisation. The differential-association theory can be applied to many types of deviant behaviour such as the group of our focal discussion. Within this theory, it is believed that juvenile gangs provide an environment in which young people learn to become criminals. These gangs define themselves as counter cultural, and glorify violence, retaliation, and for them crime may be a route to achieving social status. Gang members learn to be deviant as they embrace and conform to their gang's norms (CliffsNotes.com 2015). Consequently, the occurrence of deviant behaviour is said to be learnt from inappropriate socialisation and association. However, critics of the differential-association theory, argue that the vagueness of the theory's terminology does not lend itself to social science research methods or empirical validation (CliffsNotes.com) Regardless of such, it is not argued that deviant behaviour can violate society's norms and the given laws passed down by the upper class to the poor. As mentioned earlier most laws, crime prevention and control strategies are aimed at preserving social order. Irrespective of social norms and the laws of the land, it remains questionable, to what degree is the government successful in maintaining social order especially in reference to youth associated violent crime.

Policy and legislation on youth justice

Before 1908 the criminal justice system did not distinguish between adult and juvenile offenders. The Children Act 1908 established the principle of dealing with juvenile offenders separately from adult offenders and sent children convicted of a crime to borstals instead of prisons. Further, to this was the Children and Young Persons Act 1933 introduced a legal duty, to have regards for the welfare of the child or young person tried before them. This remains the same today. Further, to this until the intervention of Parliament (1933) the criminal responsibility of children and young persons was governed by the common law. Up until such times, a child under seven could not be held criminally responsible. Section 50 of the Children and Young Persons Act 1933 (as amended) endorsed that 'it shall be conclusively presumed that no child under the age of ten can be guilty of any offence'. (Law Mentor, 2015) Within the law there was a statutory presumption that children under the age of ten were not capable of committing a crime. This principle was encapsulated in the Latin term 'Doli incapax'. Doli incapax has been interpreted to mean 'incapacity of committing an offence'. However, the presumption of doli incapax was abolished by section 34 of the Crime and Disorder Act 1998, nevertheless the age of criminal responsibility in England and Wales remains at 10. Before the abolition of Doli incarpax, was the killing of James Bulger. By two ten year olds known as Venables and Thompson. As, they were 10 years the question of criminal responsibility came into question. At the trial, the lead prosecution counsel Richard Henriques QC successfully refuted the principle of Doli incarpax. (Foster, 1999) In this case Thompson and Venables were assessed by the court to be capable of "mischievous discretion". Which means they had an ability to act with criminal intent, and were mature enough to recognise that they were doing something seriously wrong. The child psychiatrist Dr. Eileen Vizard, who interviewed Thompson before the trial, was asked in court whether he would know the difference between right and wrong, that it was wrong to take a young child away from his mother, and that it was wrong to cause injury to a child. Vizard replied, "If the issue is on the balance of probabilities, I think I can answer with certainty". (Bulger and Dunn, n.d.) Vizard also argued that after the attack on Bulger, Thompson was suffering from post-traumatic stress disorder. Dr. Susan Bailey, a Home Office forensic psychiatrist who interviewed Venables, said unambiguously "that he knew the difference between right and wrong" (Foster 1999) Venables was also seen by a Dr from Great Ormond Street Hospital. Dr Bentovim argued, "Although Venables was chronologically over the age of

10 at the time of the killing, he was less mature as far as psychological or emotional age was concerned". Dr Bentovim went on to question, by what age do we measure responsibility - calendar dates, or emotional maturity? Between 1989 and 1991, the systems for dealing with children in need of care and those charged with criminal offences were split and the youth court created, for the trial of under-18s accused of criminal offences. However, this system isn't without its failings as was evident in the James Bulger case (1999) where the defendants' trial took place in an adult court. As a result of this trial and as recent as 2010 there has been calls to raise the age of criminal responsibility. These petitions continue to be rejected by the government (Batty, 2010) despite the fact that critics argue "we are in danger of criminalising too many children and young people" by locking them up for committing far less serious crimes" (BBC News 2010). Irrespective of the above mentioned, in 2010 the Conservatives shadow justice secretary, Dominic Grieve, argued that: "Changing the age of criminal responsibility is not the answer". He maintained that we needed fundamental reforms to address the causes of offending by children, including family breakdown, poverty, gang culture and school discipline. (BBC, 2010). Moreover, recently in 2010 we saw the conviction of two primary school boys for the attempted rape of an eight year old girl (Jones 2010). This commentator highlighted that the two boys were aged 10 years old at the time of the offence. They had been accused of repeatedly assaulting the girl in a block of flats, a lift and a bin shed before taking her to a field and raping her in October 2009. During cross-examination which took place via video link the girl admitted she had lied to her mother about the incident, and admitted that no rape had occurred. There was no other beneficial medical proof, DNA or forensic evidence (Jones 2010). All the same based on the evidence of an eight year old girl the two boys were found guilty of attempted rape. Each of the boys was sentenced to a three year supervision

order, ensuring that the boys will be under the same level of supervision as the most serious adult paedophiles. At the time this book went to publication, they are the youngest males ever to be prosecuted for rape in England and Wales. Once again as before this case was commented on. The former Director of public Prosecutions Lord Ken McDonald said "we are making demons of our children … very young children do not belong in adult courts. They rarely belong in criminal courts at all". This case once again raised the question of whether child perpetrators should be treated as adults and how old someone has to be before they have the understanding they are doing something wrong (Arthur, 2012). Further to this, the theory of criminalising children and the gargantuan number of children, in the juvenile justice system continue.

House of Commons (2013) noted that during the 1990s, the numbers of young people entering the criminal justice system, and particularly the number sentenced to custody, rose substantially. In 1996 the Audit Commission published Misspent Youth: Young People and Crime, which found that there was no integrated youth justice system and the system was inefficient and ineffective. This report was the driving force behind the much needed changes, to the structures and framework for how professionals responded to offending by children and young people (under 18's). As noted earlier the Crime and Disorder Act 1998 defined the primary aim of the youth justice system in preventing offending by children and young people'. Further, to this The Crime and Disorder Act placed a duty on every local authority to establish and fund a multi-agency youth offending team in their area (YOT), which would be responsible for coordinating youth justice provision. All YOT teams must be inclusive of representatives from the police, probation, health, education and children's services to work with children and young people offending or on the periphery of offending. Further, to this YOTs have a continued responsibility and a duty of care for children and young people sentenced or remanded to custody (Public Health England 2013).

At national level, a Youth Justice Board (YJB) was established to monitor and advise the Secretary of State in relation to the youth justice system. However, the success of the YJB was questioned by the Coalition government 2011 who threatened to abolish it. However, the then Justice secretary Kenneth Clark had to do a U-turn on this decision in advance of an expected House of Lords defeat over the move (Travis and Khan, 2011). The Crime and Disorder Act 1998, and subsequent legislation, also made significant changes to the sentences and out-of-court disposals available for dealing with young offenders. It is the case that the last seventeen years have seen some minor changes within the youth justice system, however the extent of the Department of Education involvement has varied (House of Commons Justice Committee 2012/13) once again calling into question the ability, commitment and equality of the education system in preparing the youth of today for the leaders of tomorrow.

It was noted earlier that the incidence of gun-related crime, killings, injures, and intimidation, are frequently linked to youth gang activity and the illegal drugs trade in the UK. These incidences amongst others such as the killing of James Bulger by two children who were later named as Venables and Thompson have the capability of causing moral panic. It cannot be disputed that after each incident where a youth -young person loses their life, it is normally followed by a media coverage which will often provoke anger and public repugnance. However, although the media were very active in the Bulger case, all press coverage on the new identities given to Venables and Thompson were prohibited. However, the incidence of guns and gangs has received no such restrictions but has led to various government initiatives which have been aimed at tackling gun crime and safeguarding the safety and security of British society. In so doing not only was there the ratification of the Crime and Disorder Act 1998, we have also seen the endorsement of various disposals available to the courts which are inclusive of, referral orders, youth rehabilitation order, a detention and training order for those over 12 years and under 18 years. There is also a minimum five-year sentence for people convicted of possessing an illegal firearm. However, where the offender is aged 16 or 17 at the time of the offence and under 18 at the date of conviction this given sentence (5 years) is reduced to 3 years detention under section 91 of the Powers of Criminal Courts (Sentencing Act 2000. S29 (3) (b) and s29 (6) (Crown Prosecution Service 2007).

However, the minimum 5 years imprisonment will apply to offenders aged 18 or over at the time of conviction (Crown Prosecution Service 2007). In addition, we have also seen the ratification of The Violent Crime Reduction Act 2006, which includes:

Targeting imitation firearms – by making it illegal to manufacture or sell imitation firearms that could be mistaken for real firearms, strengthening sentences for carrying imitation firearms, and creating tougher manufacturing standards so imitations can't be converted to fire real ammunition. Over the years these interventions have proved very expensive for the public purse. The Committee of Public accounts (2011) noted that "During 2009-2010 Central government and local authorities spent £800 million in dealing with youth crime, primarily through the Youth Justice Board nationally and Youth Offending Teams locally". Of this budget ten per cent was spent on trying to prevent young people becoming offenders. The rest of the spending was incurred whilst dealing with offending behaviour. Over £300 million was spent on those in custody (the secure estate). The National Audit Office estimated that the total costs to the UK economy of offending by young people could be up to £11 billion a year (The Committee of Public Accounts 2011).

As a result of published data, the question remains could this money be better spent and if so how?

Education and the youth justice system

The education system has always been a driver of social policies. Its primary purpose is to develop each individual to their fullest potential, imparting the knowledge of social norms and values as well as preparing a work force that is able to contribute to the economy. In recent years we have seen the education system dealing with much more than education and social norms, but also with the impact of depravation and family segregation. This state of affairs, may have been to the detriment of the BME (specifically black boys). For some time now the extent to which the education system is failing black boys has been a topic of debate in various government departments and the media. In 2002 the Labour MP Diane Abbott told the Guardian Newspaper, "There is a silent catastrophe happening in Britain's schools in the way they continue to fail black British school-children". She further argued "this is not a new issue. As long ago as 1977 a House of Commons select committee on race relations and immigration reported that 'as a matter of urgency the Government should institute a high-level and independent inquiry into the causes of the underachievement of children of West Indian origin in maintained schools (Abbott, 2002). Irrespective of the call for an independent inquiry by the select committee in 1977, as highlighted by Ms Abbott in 2002, thirty years and six years later respectively the headlines read: Black Caribbean children held back by institutional racism in schools (Curtis, 2008). A study published in the Guardian showed that:

> ➤ A third of the most capable black Caribbean pupils are not entered to take the hardest papers in tests at 14

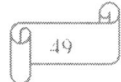

> Black Caribbean and mixed white-and-black Caribbean children are excluded at rates three times greater than that for white children.

The study further revealed that:

> In 2007 44.9% of black Caribbean pupils, and 47.3% of pupils of mixed white and black Caribbean heritage, achieved 5 or more A*-C grades, compared to 57.3%nationally

> The gap between black Caribbean achievement and the national average at GCSE has narrowed by eight percentage points in four years. By the same token it was disturbing to learn that in 2005 there were twice as many black men in prison in the UK than in universities (Curtis, 2008).

In recognition of the aforesaid, it is important to establish, if there is a link between the publicly criticised education system, and the incidence of crime?

In looking at young offenders' and guns and gangs, it is important to address education or the lack thereof and the incidence of crime. Curtis (2008) noted that many "Black Caribbean children were held back by institutional racism in schools". My research did not uncover a reason why black children are subjected to a bigotry institution. However when looking for reasons of disproportionate exclusion and underachievement one thing that stands out is children been labelled as naughty and disruptive.

An article by Garner (2009) read Children are being labelled "naughty" as a result of their teachers' views of their home backgrounds. This publication further highlighted that once children are tagged as troublesome it is difficult to shake that reputation off. Garners article focused on a study that was commissioned by the

Economic and Social Research Council, which looked at the behaviour of children aged four and five in reception classes. This early age tagging is indicative of how children are judged from an early age. In direct harmony of the aforementioned, Gillborn (1990, qtd in Majors 2001) argued that amid all the challenges that were faced by black children in the education system they must also develop strategies to handle white teachers assumptions that they are likely to cause disruption. This pre-judgemental viewpoint automatically causes a disadvantage for the said student where uncontrollable, unacceptable behaviour is expected.

One will acknowledge that bad behaviour and violence in schools is totally unacceptable, and as such there needs to be a mechanism for dealing with it. The incidence of challenging and unacceptable behaviour it is often dealt by way of exclusion either permanent or temporary which the institute usually deems as fitting. However, in reality, this exclusion may have an impact that goes far beyond the school gates affecting the local communities, local businesses, victims of crime and social services etc. Gilbertson (cited at Donovan et al.) highlighted that in 1996 an audit commission found "42% of offenders of school age who are sentenced in the youth court had been excluded from school". Further to this, it was argued by Rod Morgan, (previous Chair of the Youth Justice Board): that "We know children excluded from school are much more likely to commit crime and anti-social behaviour" (Youth Justice Board online). This theory was supported by Malins (Conservative party 2009) during a speech where he acknowledged "at school, some young people get behind and begin to fail, consequently they cannot keep up with their peers and get angry and bad-tempered". "When things go wrong, they are excluded because of their poor performance, and they are out on the streets, where they commit crimes, which leads to them being locked up". If we are prepared to accept these statements, it would show a correlation between the levels of literacy and school exclusions, and between school exclusions and crime. However, this argument was disputed by Gilbertson (cited at Donovan et al. online) who concludes that although there are opportunities to offend if a child is in an unstructured environment, there is no evidence that there is a clear causal relationship between exclusion from school and juvenile offending. However research carried out by the University of Edinburgh and published in 2013 argued that "Pupils excluded from school at 12 are four times more likely than other children to be jailed as adults". The researchers further highlighted that boys, living in single parent families, and those from the poorest communities were most likely to be excluded from school. This report also acknowledged that other pupils who displayed the same level of poor behaviour, but were from more affluent areas, and those from two parent families were afforded a greater level of tolerance and, as a result, were far less likely to be expelled from school (The University of Edinburgh, 2013). With the published result and the ongoing deliberations, is it possible to conclusively say there is a correlation between school exclusion and the incidence? This is a debate that may persist for some time. However, what may not be debatable is the fact that an exclusion from school has a knock on effect which is holistic in its affects.

The revelations of these finding will come as no surprise to many. However, what may be surprising is the knock-on effect that low attainment and a lack of motivation, coupled with external factors, such as money, designer cloths and an impoverished standard of living has on the lives of young people. In deliberation of the above and coupled with the impediment created by the education system, it raises the question of "are black boys choosing to decline an institutionally bigoted education structure, for a fraternity where instant gratification" is given priority over long term gain?

It is noted that the effects of deprivation can display itself in many shapes and forms inclusive of anti-social behaviour. Further to this it may be the case that the above mentioned circumstances (isolation, lack of encouragement and motivation) may have contributed to Schools having to deal with young people's anti-social actions, and the rise and aftermath of violent crimes, which not only impacted on their peers but has affected professionals in the line of their duty, for example the unfortunate fatal stabbing of a head teacher, Phillip Lawrence (1995) (News.bbc.co.uk, 2005)

With an open mind the reader may agree that the young people who are caught up in delinquent behaviour, are the future of the country. Accordingly, it should be the case that they are adapting to social norms and being prepared for the workforce and their economic contribution to society. However, it is an alarming reality that we are heading for a generation of socially excluded young men (and women to a lesser degree) who will spend a substantial amount of their lives in prison. In November 2006 there were 11,862 under 21 year old in prison this figure includes 2,841 under 18's and 15% of this total number is represented by black or black British. A study carried out by the Guardian in 2011 found that nothing much had changed. Ball, Boycott and Rogers (2011) found that black offenders were 44% more likely than white offenders to be sentenced to prison for driving offences, 38% more likely to be imprisoned for public disorder or possession of a weapon and 27% more likely for drugs possession. They further argued that Asian offenders were 41% more likely to be -sent to prison for drugs offences than their white counterparts and 19% more likely to go to jail for shoplifting. This data raises the question of how equal is the youth justice system and how deep does institutional racism run, stacking the cards against malcontent children and young people.

The aforesaid data has and continues to have an impact on the country's economy in terms of the money paid to keep children and young people in custody. It is believed that in 2003/04 it cost £36,000 to keep an individual in custody, coupled with this is the cost of separated families, social exclusion, and a massive impact on a dying skilled workforce. Knuutila (2010) noted that the cost of holding a person in a Young Offender institution (YOI) has risen substantially over the years, costing about £100,000 a year.

Social exclusion the criminalizing of children, and children in care

Today around a quarter of all offenders are between ten and seventeen years old. The Home Office research paper on youth crime in England and Wales in 2009/10 shows that youngsters commit a 'disproportionate' amount of crime. This paper further revealed that under-18s make up a tenth of the population but are responsible for 23 per cent of offences (Doyle, 2012). It may be argued that in part the criminal activities and the criminalisation of this groups of young people, who are from poorer backgrounds, can be attributed to a lack of affordable organised leisure activities.

In many working class communities' leisure activities, which were mostly associated with youth clubs have been disbanded, music studios can be costly and any other pastime activity are scarce, having been cut by government and local councils budget cuts. These cuts have left many working class young people with little alternative but to meet up with friends, and hang around the streets and estates in groups, looking for something to do. However, due to public perception and media coverage, some adults find the presence of such groups menacing (Williams,

2008). I can be suggested that fear experienced may be attributed in part to the division of the classes, ageism and social exclusion.

Further to the above, other children in need of services, whether it be leisure or otherwise, are the children who come into contact with the welfare and the criminal justice system. There is no denying that some of the concerns which bring children and families to the attention of the local authority can be appalling, recent examples have been baby P (Wardrop, 2010) and Victoria Climbie (Batty, 2002). However the negative effects of the given concerns which brought theses children and family to the attention of social services, can be further exasperated by the experience of cooperate parenting, and the lack of experience knowledge and understanding of what is required of them as was identified by the failings of baby P. Additional and of equal concern is the large number of children in care, who are involved in the criminal justice system. The Centre for Social Justice (2008) noted "research has shown children who have been in care account for 49% of the 11,672 under 21 year olds' in contact with the criminal justice system (Robson 2008)". Further, to this, it was also noted that, over half of those under 18 in custody have a history of being in care or have experienced social services involvement. Notwithstanding this, children who are looked after by the local authority often suffer from isolation. A report produced by County Durham, (All the lonely people: social isolation and loneliness in County Durham, 2015) highlighted that "looked after children and care leavers Young people in or leaving care are more likely to experience difficulties regarding social integration if established support networks are not in place. They are more likely to have faced multiple disadvantages such as poverty, poor family relationships, rejection, disruption and loss in their lives. Subsequent life-chances, including outcomes closely related to social isolation such as mental health problems, low educational attainment and worklessnesss are significantly influenced by these experiences. In a nutshell isolation for them refers to separation from social or familial contact, community involvement, or access to services. Moreover it is argued that "the idea of social exclusion builds on the long-standing recognition that material exclusion is both caused by, and is a cause of, exclusion from other domains related to an individual's wellbeing. Social exclusion is generally accepted to be a multifaceted concept involving more than simply material disadvantage (Kneale, 2012). Hence, it can be concluded that Social exclusion not only refers to economic hardship or relative economic poverty, but is presented as a multifaceted problem. It is related to poverty, and the understanding of poverty which can go far beyond low income and relative deprivation. Poverty and social exclusion may be systematically separated, with poverty being the lack of material resources, especially income, necessary to participate in society, and relative deprivation is being deprived of something one believes they are entitled to for example the need for decent housing and a reasonable income. Many children and young people in prison have a background of severe social exclusion poverty and deprivation. It may then be argued that the lack of local economic resources, social networks, the impact of unemployment and varying education issues may all play a role in the quality and quantity and persistence of youth crime. Poverty and deprivation can often have an impact on family life and sometimes this can lead to children being taken into care.

Deprivation experienced by youth and its impact

For many years it has been suggested that poverty is closely tied to crime. However, the question remains, does poverty cause crime, or are some other triggers, such as dysfunctional families, and a lack of community solidity able to explain why some families experiences both poverty and criminality?

Evidence published by The Centre for Social Justice, (2009) seems to argue that the emergence of gangs that are semi-organised, violent criminal are born out of acute deprivation. They also acknowledge that the gap between the rich and the poor is increasing, consequently there are more people living in severe poverty today than a decade ago. Breakthrough Britain, (cited at The Centre for Social Justice) identifies the drivers of poverty as being family breakdown, failed education, addiction, debt and generational worklessnesss. Their published findings, which are said to impact youth behaviour were broken down in the following way:

Family breakdowns:

More than half the babies born to British mothers will have been born out of marriage

- Nearly one in 2 cohabiting parents split up before their child's 5th birthday, compared to 1 in 12 married parents

- ¾ of family breakdown affecting young children now involves unmarried parents

- If you have experienced family breakdown you are 75% more likely to fail at school, 70% more likely to be a drug addict and 50% more likely to have alcohol problems

For many years there has been an ongoing debate as to the impacts of growing up in poverty, on later life behaviour. Griggs and Walker (2008) noted that an association

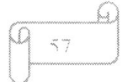

between childhood poverty and behavioural outcomes is evident from an early age. They further argued that "those who grow up in low-income households, have a greater likelihood of parents reporting behavioural concerns than their more affluent counterparts". It was noted earlier, that these children are more likely to be excluded from school which will often lead to social exclusion, which in turn may impact on displayed behaviours. Notwithstanding this, it is further suggested that as these children get older more concerns will be raised which include risk-taking behaviour, aggression, and involvement in crime (Griggs and Walker, 2008 p. 5). However it is argued that there remains extensive disparity over whether crime can be considered a by-product of childhood poverty, with US studies more likely to identify a direct relationship, and UK research highlighting the complexity of the association. Therefore it may be reasonable to surmise that most children raised in poverty do not become involved in crime, nevertheless there is a higher number of victims and the fear of crime in disadvantaged areas.

The opinion that poverty causes crime is often taken for granted. However, it needs to be remembered that crime is committed for a variety of reasons by the rich as well as the poor, with no offence been unique to any given group. In spite of this, in a progressively unequal society, the poor are penalized more, not just in the criminal justice system, but equally by society. This position is clear from the decisions taken in recent years by the government.

In recent years (2010-2015) the UK was governed by a coalition government. Part of their manifesto was to cut public spending. The impact of their austerity program, is hardest on those people most depend on support from public services and social security, according to a new study from the New Economics Foundation think tank. The Think Tank further argued that the impact of this austerity means that those who are poor and powerless have less time and fewer resources at their disposal (Slay and Penny, 2013). This in turn may have a detrimental impact on parents who may already be struggling to spend quality time with and socialise their children, which then calls their parenting skills and commitment into question, thus adding to an already negative picture, that society has of these families, which in turn further adds to the pressures of trying to conform to social norm, deprivation, social exclusion and a question of parenting capacity, which further leads these parents performance open to speculation and question of good enough parenting.

Good enough parenting by whose standard

Parenting and parenting styles are often the topic of discussion amongst social workers and care professionals even more so after the recent child deaths. This conversation will often arise due to a child or young person coming to the attention of the police or social services. More often than not, judgments without any substance will be made about the background of the family, the home of the young person and parenting capability of the parents.

For many years developmental psychologists have looked at how parenting capabilities can have an impact on a child's development. Nonetheless, finding actual causal effects and links between specific actions of parents and later behaviour of children has proven difficult. In spite of these challenges, research has uncovered substantial links between parenting styles and the effects these styles have on children. During the early 1960s, psychologist Diana Baumrind conducted a study on more than 100 preschool-age children. During her inquires she identified four styles of parenting which were as follows:

1. Authoritarian Parenting

In this style of parenting, children are expected to follow the strict rules established by the parents. Failure to follow such rules usually results in punishment. Authoritarian parents fail to explain the reasoning behind these rules. If asked to explain, the parent might simply reply, "Because I said so." These parents have high demands of, but are not responsive to their children. According to Baumrind, these parents "are obedience- and status-oriented, and expect their orders to be obeyed without explanation" (1991).

2. Authoritative Parenting

Like authoritarian parents, those with an authoritative parenting style create rules and guidelines that their children are expected to follow. Nevertheless, this parenting style is much more democratic. Authoritative parents are reactive to the needs of their children and willing to listen to questions. When children fail to meet their expectations, these parents are more nurturing and forbearing rather than punishing.

Baumrind suggests that authoritative parents "observes and instil clear standards to regulate their children's behaviour. They are assertive, but not intrusive and restrictive. Their disciplinary approaches are supportive, rather than punitive. They want their children to be confident as well as socially responsible, and self-regulated as well as cooperative" (Grobman, 2008).

3. Permissive Parenting

Permissive parenting, is sometimes referred to as indulgent parenting. It is said that these parents make few demands of their children. It was believed that these parents seldom discipline their children as they have somewhat low expectations of their maturity and self-control. According to Baumrind, permissive parents "are more responsive to their children than they are demanding". They are non-traditional, tolerant, and do not require mature behaviour, allow considerable self-regulation, and avoid confrontation. Permissive parents are usually nurturing and communicative with their children, frequently taking on the role of an acquaintance more than that of a parent. Kendra Cherry 2015)

4. Uninvolved Parenting (which was added at a later date)

An involved parenting style is characterized by few demands, low responsiveness and little communication. While these parents fulfil the child's basic needs, they are generally detached from their child's life. In extreme cases, these parents may even reject or neglect the needs of their children. (Kendra Cherry 2015)

The aforesaid has shown there to be four styles of parenting. However Cherry argues that the research into parenting styles isn't without its limitations, thus no two parents will parent their children in the same way even if they are using the same style of parenting. As a result, we may still ask, why do parenting styles differ? In answer to that question it may be necessary to look at the impact and influences of culture, personality of the parents, the background and history of parents and how they were parented, family size, socioeconomic status, educational level, religion and the input of the extended family.

Further to this Katz, et al (2007) argued "it is also important to note that parents have their own needs as adults and assessments of the relationship between poverty and parenting ought to take a holistic view of parents' lives". They concluded that "most existing studies of poor families have tended to focus on parenting practices and style in relation to parental employment" (Katz, et al., 2007).

Has the old proverb "it takes a village to raise a child" disappeared?

The ancient proverb of "it takes a village to raise a child" implies that no man, woman, or family is an island and we all have a responsibility to each other. This theory goes back to biblical days. Genesis 4:8-11, tells us that when they were in the field, that Cain rose up against Abel his brother and killed him. Then the LORD said to Cain, "Where is Abel your brother?" And Cain said, "I do not know. Am I my brother's keeper?" Jesus said, "What have you done"? "The voice of your brother's blood is crying to Me from the ground" (Bible Gateway N/D)..... However, in these days, our families and communities are not what they should be. We would like to think that we live in a society where people care about others -- where people join forces helping when things get tough -- where it is safe to leave your door unlocked and your children can play safely outside, where your children are known in the neighbourhood and everyone taking a caring interest in their welfare.

However, this is far from what is experienced. Instead of community collaboration, we are often isolated; and one of the consequences of this is, crime is a major part of our community and community collaboration is at an all-time low. Many parents hoped for a better life for our children, one which was far removed from the days of the Windrush. However, what is true is that we have encountered gangs and drugs, which have been propelled by lies, cover ups and a fragmented community where people retreat behind closed. Legislators focus on the incidence of crime as part of their manifesto and vote winner, the older generation are disheartened at the lack of union and togetherness in raising our children, and often ask " where is the village-community around the child is"? Sadly, the village and community support are inadequate.

In society today individuals are occupied with their own issues which consist of deprivation, unemployment, debt, other family challenges, and a lack of community cohesion, these coupled with a deficiency in the level of support, from those in power, has eroded cultural and family values, thus parents are struggling to provide parenting in a manner that meets the needs of their families and community.

Family and parental support which is culturally focused

There are many factors which need to be taken into account when working with service users from an ethnic minority background, and one of the biggest ones are the culture match, cultural mismatch and cultural awareness. Furthermore, it is the case and rarely acknowledged that the cultural identity, experiences, attitudes and prejudices of a social worker may impact on their ability to engage in a positive way with this service group. Consequently, the relationship between families and services providers are far from what is needed or required. Parents and families require services that are reliable, available, sensitive to individual needs, dependable and co-ordinated. A service which understands their history, their struggles in terms of isolation, cultural parenting and the need to be a provider for their family daily which in itself is a struggle. In addition, it is questionable whether parents and families in need, are able to engage with and build trusting relationships with the front-line service providers, and to what degree parents feel they are in control, of the help they are receiving. It is the case that many agencies provide a targeted cultural service for example Barnardos (Reaching families in need, 2011). It is fundamental to note, that in-order to understand and address the issues that persist around youth anti-social behaviour, and the lack of

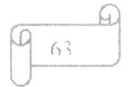

parent engagement, a culturally focused service that doesn't just pay lip service, will need to be a priority for local authority service providers (social services).

Bad company kill's good characters, and as such these young people will often become involved in the following behavours in an attempt to be accepted or protected

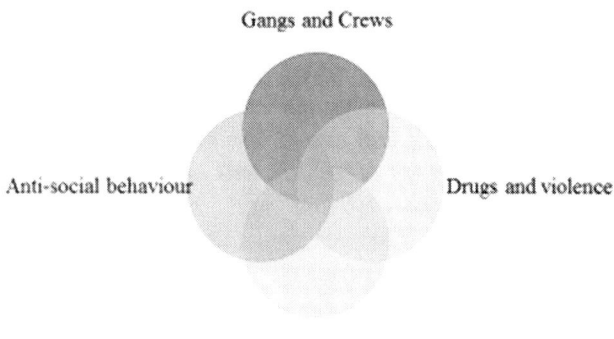

Gangs and Crews

Anti-social behaviour

Drugs and violence

Truanting

Over the years what we have learnt from young people in gangs is that they are very into what they term as street cred and for them this means;

1. The protection of own turf (this used to be postcode)

2. Defending of each other (ride or die)

3. Wearing of name brand clothes and their gang colors which will be their gang identity

4. Communicating in their own/street language

5. Friends holding them in high admiration/martyr

Accordingly, many young people are prepared to lose their life in the name of street cred (dead with street cred).

When a young person is killed, it may be the case (in the eyes of their friends) that they died with street cred they are seen as a hero.

Regardless of this myth, what is true is that with the death of each young person we have a victim an offender and the least two broken families.

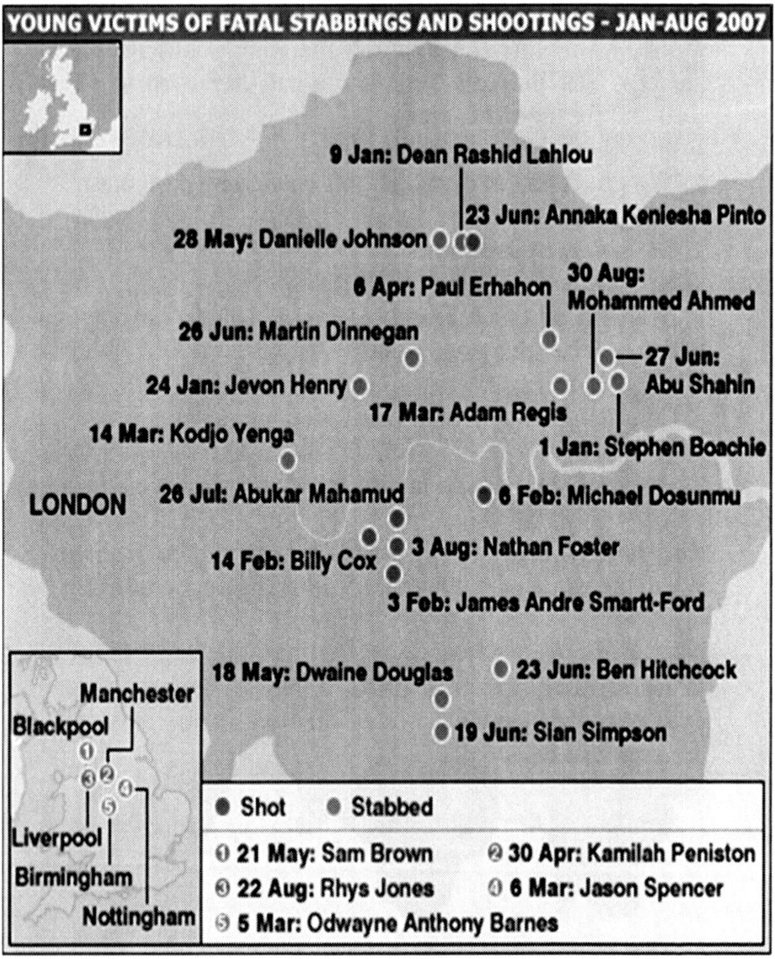

YOUNG VICTIMS OF FATAL STABBINGS AND SHOOTINGS - JAN-AUG 2007

9 Jan: Dean Rashid Lahlou

23 Jun: Annaka Keniesha Pinto

28 May: Danielle Johnson

6 Apr: Paul Erhahon

30 Aug: Mohammed Ahmed

26 Jun: Martin Dinnegan

27 Jun: Abu Shahin

24 Jan: Jevon Henry

17 Mar: Adam Regis

14 Mar: Kodjo Yenga

1 Jan: Stephen Boachie

LONDON

26 Jul: Abukar Mahamud

6 Feb: Michael Dosunmu

14 Feb: Billy Cox

3 Aug: Nathan Foster

3 Feb: James Andre Smartt-Ford

18 May: Dwaine Douglas

23 Jun: Ben Hitchcock

Manchester

19 Jun: Sian Simpson

Blackpool

① ②

Liverpool

Birmingham

Nottingham

● Shot ● Stabbed

① 21 May: Sam Brown   ② 30 Apr: Kamilah Peniston
③ 22 Aug: Rhys Jones   ④ 6 Mar: Jason Spencer
⑤ 5 Mar: Odwayne Anthony Barnes

---

26 teenagers were killed in London in 2007.

A murder victim does not amount to a gang member, but it does amount to several broken families:

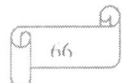

Stop the Killing begin the healing

James Smartt-Ford, Michael Dosunmu, Billy Cox,
Kodjo Yenga, Adam Regis, Paul Erhahon,
Annaka Pinto, Ben Hitchcock, Martin Dinnegan

Although, he may not have been part of a gang at the time of his death, Shakilus Townsend was beaten by a gang of at least 5 youths in Thornton Heath London on the 4th July 2008. When this young man was killed the headlines read "Shakilus Townsend, 16, lured into London knife murder ambush by teenage girl". This headline soon became "The Honey Trap killing". The young people involved in this horrific crime received sentences totaling 87 years (minimum). (News Shopper, 2009) In reference to the previous paragraph, we had a victim, several perpetrators and at least eight broken families. Due to the impact of this occurrence, the effected families are going to have various requirements which need to be met not only by the police, housing, health care services but also by social workers. In order to be suitably equipped, not only to meet the need of the offender, their families inclusive of any siblings, and any   victim, you should be aware of what "Dead with street cred" mean to you as an intercession worker

Social workers need specialist exposure and training.

Over the years the attention given to social workers by the media has been very negative. Social workers often lack the skills to work and engage with children and young people with challenging behaviour, those involved in gangs and the victim of gangs, is a theory supported by Sir Martin Narey, (Harrison, 2014). The world of social work, within the children and families team, can be very formidable for a social worker, who has no knowledge or understanding of this service user group. For those of you who are familiar with the story of Daniel in the bible, you will know that he was thrown into the lion's den for his beliefs in God (Daniel 7 v 16). The bible tells us that God preserved Daniels life. This scenario has been thrown in

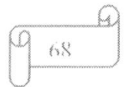

here, as often social workers are required to deal with young people, who display challenging behaviours and those in gangs. Without an understanding of the history, demographics of the area, and the challenges before you, it can feel as though you have been thrown into the lion's den. In 2014 Sir Martin Narey, the former head of the prison service in England and Wales and the charity Barnardo's, advises the Education Secretary Michael Gove on children's social care that Social work training needs upgrading. He further commented that standards were "variable" and many employers thought graduates were sometimes inadequately prepared for "the challenge of children's social work" (Harrison, 2014)

Welcoming Sir Naey's report, the Education Secretary said "too many social workers are leaving university today ill-prepared for their vital role working to protect at risk children." (The Rt Hon Michael Gove MP 2014, cited at Department for Education, 2014) Notwithstanding this, the House of Commons Children, Schools and Families Committee, further highlighted that when social workers are poorly trained—lacking in knowledge, skills, or experience—or left unsupported in highly pressured situations, children's lives are put in danger. It is equally important to declare that an ill prepared social workers could be putting their own lives in danger. As a result, it is imperative to have an understanding of the service user, the demographics of the working area, the gangs, their make-up and the corollaries of dead with street cred, and its implications for you as a worker. As a social worker within the children-in-need department, you will be faced with many unique challenges, but none as challenging as young people in gangs who will often seek revenge for a friend who has been killed. 'Dead with street cred' may have a sinister meaning to the 'gangs', but can provide a social worker with assistance as it will keep you focused on the task at hand

What does DEAD with STREET CRED mean to us?

- D= DETECT
- E= ENGAGE
- A= ASSIST
- D= DETER

                    With Street

- C= CRIME
- R= REDUCTION
- E= ENVIROMENTAL
- D= DESIGN

Guns and gangs, whose responsibility are they anyway

The present and past Governments have failed to stop the surge of gangs and their impact. But we ask whose responsibility is it anyway?

The absence of strong and committed leadership shown by central and local Government has meant that we in the UK have failed to understand and act on the increasing problem of street gangs. In many communities, tackling gangs has been seen as the responsibility of the police by politicians who have made enforcement their primary focus and taken a punitive position without much success. In spite of the evidently mounting problem with gang activity, and violence over the past decade, it took community and media reproof, before the government created a strategy for confronting gangs and gang

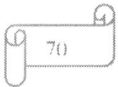

70

activities. Irrespective of the Government's strategy and its publication guide on 'Tackling Gangs', (Home Office 2008) there remains a number of key issues which continued to strike at the foundations of any attempt to tackle Britain's gang culture which were and still are inclusive of Poor leadership and guidance at the most senior levels in central and local government, poor organisation and information sharing between agencies and a failure to communicate with gang-entrenched communities over a sustained period. What's more, the powers that be have viewed it more important to concentrated on the physical restoration of the infrastructure of a community (this was evident with the London riots of 2011) without physically, mentally or emotionally impacting on the lives of those who reside within the buildings. The Government has maintained that they want to address the given issues created by the gangs, however poor resourcing and support of grass roots charities tackling the drivers, pushers and symptoms of gang culture remain an issue (The Centre for Social Justice)

As noted, resourcing and support to grass root organisations has become very scarce over time, thus, suitably qualified services who are able to engage and interact with these children and young people have been destabilised. In addition to the above mentioned, children and young people who are members of gangs are often known to numerous statutory agencies, however the ability of the local authorities to engage and deal with the persisting problem of gangs as part of their statutory safeguarding children duties remains questionable, as there seems to be no documented evidence on their success. Coupled with this is an ongoing failure to communicate and share data, which can have rippling affects.

The introduction of this book, looked at the rise of the 'gangs'. This document focused mainly on afro-Caribbean men who were classed as gang members and predominantly responsible for black on black crime. In an attempt to deal with the aforementioned issues Metropolitan Police Trident department was established Camber, 2010). Coupled together these two factors seem to indicate that we have an issue with black boys and young black men in society today. However, this was not always the case. If you are fortunate to speak to a great-grandparents, or even a great-great grandparent, who came to the UK as part of the Windrush they tell a different story. The mass immigration of black people from the Caribbean to Britain started with the Windrush in 1948. It is argued that "the Windrush generation were in many ways failed by a nation which ostensibly rejected them and spurned their offspring". It is further argued that they were "failed by an educational system which unjustly and erroneously labelled their sons and daughters as nothing more than troublemakers and natural athletes, and in so doing tragically placed a limit on their achievements, by telling them that they would never amount to much more than footballers, singers or athletes" (Afroeurope.blogspot.co.uk, 2013). Regardless of how they were treated, they stayed and had their children, children who were raise in loving homes. Furthermore they would tell you that, children of past generations, didn't behave in this lawless manner. They were raised by the family, both immediate and extended, well-mannered, suitably disciplined, and respectful to adults and authority. They further commented that in the Caribbean, the way that they raised their children, was very different to how children are raised in the UK, and with the interference of the Government, and these people they call 'social services', children no longer have any manners, respect, or a healthy fear of authority, which is inclusive of their parents. (Anonymous grandparent 2009). Anonymous grandparent explained "Our culture has been eroded , we need to follow the laws of the land, they talk about norms and equal rights, but, the is no equal rights for our grandchildren, their life conditions are worse than when my parents and the continuous interference of the Government has a lot to answer for". Notwithstanding this, it is acknowledged by a lot of parents who were born to Caribbean parents that as children they were often 'beaten' by their parents. Now they laugh about how they were disciplined, however, they were loved, cared for and provided for.

When we look at the reference made to beaten as stated above, s58 of the Children Act 1989 relates to crucial, and although it would be hard to deny that there was no need for this piece of legislation, it is equally hard to disagree with those who say that the government interference of the government has impacted on their ability to reasonably discipline their children, and now their children are out of control, killing each other in the name of 'Street Cred' the only discipline which is on offer is that handed down by a institutionally bigoted criminal justice system.

Young people and consequential thinking

Many young people who are involved in anti-social behaviour fail to apply consequential thinking or victim empathy to their actions or behaviour. This group can be very calculating in their actions, however, the consideration of what 'if' which seem to be very low on their list of concerns. As such, it may be deemed appropriate to teach consequential thinking at school and from a very early age. Consequential thinking is not just applicable to youth and crime, as it is so vigorously applied today, but should be applied to the educational curriculum as soon as children are able to understand the legal definition of right and wrong. The age of criminal responsibility in England and Wales is 10 years old, and as such consequential thinking should be taught at this age. Further, to this there are many programs which discourage criminal behaviour such as KeepOut, a Crime Diversion scheme run at Coldingley prison. KeepOut is a unique programme aimed at preventing youth crime. This programme which was launched in 1996 was as one of the first crime diversion scheme to be delivered by dedicated teams of serving prisoners. Prisoners are trained by KeepOut to run intervention programs for young people that inform, support and divert those between 13 and 17 who are either at risk of entering the criminal justice system or are already involved in criminal activity (Crimediversionscheme.org.uk, 2011). It is often the case that many young people who have never been to prison are inclined to glorify it, and view it as a 'holiday camp. However, a visit to Coldingley will show the harsh reality of prison life for young people who offend and are sentenced to custody, thus allowing for reflection of their behaviour, and the application of consequential thinking

A reactive approach versus a proactive approach

It may be argued, and to a greater extent agreed, that the youth justice system, in dealing with the incidence of youth crime and anti-social behaviour, is one that is reactive, with its best defence being incarceration, and other inadequate policy and procedures. The reactive approach by the government is evident when they continue to miss opportunities for prevention in the early lives, and school experiences of children. In the past these missed opportunities have, and still contribute to the high numbers of young people in custody, the high YOT case loads, and the high recidivism rates. Successive government have continued to experiment with various anti-social policies for example dispersal orders and ASBO's.

Sections 30-36 of the Anti-Social Behaviour Act 2003 (ASBA) came into force in 2003 and gave the police forces in England and Wales new powers which included authority to disperse groups of two or more people from areas where there is persistent anti-social behaviour. This Anti-social Behaviour Act was replaced on 20 October 2014, with sections 34 - 42 of the Anti-social Behaviour, Crime and Policing Act 2014. The new dispersal power replaces those available under section 30 of the ASBA 2003 and section 27 of the Violent Crime Reduction Act 2006 (The Crown Prosecution Service 2014) Nevertheless, the subcultures in which juvenile crime thrives, appears to be nonreactive to the various legislations, law enforcement agencies and the ramifications of the punitive system. As a result, it has been increasingly recognised that the powers or lack thereof, of the traditional youth justice organization, does not effectually control crime, consequently it is essential to procure the cooperation of the community and those organisations at grass roots level, who are capable and able to achieve positive outcomes with the appropriate funding and support. Furthermore, it is imperative that the government looks closely reducing the numbers of young people in custody, (both sentenced and remands) whilst still keeping the community safe. It is suggested an alternative to custody, necessitating a focus on the drivers behind youth crime, without the dogmatic punitive measures may be an alternative. One such programme which aims to address this is the Daphne programme. The Daphne programme highlighted the positive outcomes which could be obtained by using intensive foster care for those on remand as an alternative to custody (BAAF, 2014).

It is profoundly crucial for those in government who are able to have an impact on youth crime and the juvenile justice system, to conscientiously give consideration to the causalities and relationships on the lives of those who become involved in crime in order to find a lasting solution. It is imperative that the government revisits the long-standing hypotheses which have signpost the roads to the incidence of youth crime, such as deprivation, poverty, education, socialization and the causes of instant gratification, such as media influences.

Every five years more than any other time, youth crime is top priority, it is included in every parties manifesto, and every government vows to address the issues of poverty, unemployment and youth crime. They review their policies with an intent of addressing these issues. However, how successful they have been is questionable. Policies implemented in the last ten years have included Every Child Matters, the Crime and Disorder Act, Crime Reduction Partnership, the London Anti-Social Behaviour Strategy and the Prolific and other Priority offenders Strategy to name but a few. Social policies are about addressing social issues. Delinquent behaviour is a big social issue at present, as it touches many parts of society, impacting on social norms and social work practices. Social workers are now involved not only in respect to safe guarding children, but also in the criminal justice system.

One of the oldest policies and legislation is the Children's Act. This policy was aimed at protecting the child and assisting the family. In 1889 the first act of parliament was passed, called The Prevention of Cruelty to Children... It has been reviewed at significant times throughout the years with the first Children Act been enacted in 1908 and then in 1989, with the most recent review/addition been in 2004/2005 in line with Every Child Matters and the Department for Education and Skills to name a few. The revision of the given Acts demands more joined up/mufti agency working and out of the box thinking. The benefits of joint up –multi-agency working will allow, the social worker to be more advantageous not only with reference to protecting children, but also with holistic assessment been done and family intervention been carried out which are culturally focused, and not management or budget driven.

Over the last two decades we have seen social workers placed in court teams, Youth Offending Teams, secure establishments, young offender's institutes and local authority secure children's homes. Theoretically, by placing social workers in these services, they are advantageously placed to begin, engaging, encouraging and assisting child/young people in their reflective - consequential thinking, also to reach the five outcomes which were established by the Every Childs Matters and Changes for Children agendas. These outcomes were considered a necessity for well-being in childhood and later in adulthood and are as follows:

1. Being Healthy

2. Staying Safe

3. Enjoying and achieving

4. Making a positive contribution

5. Economic well-being

When the Coalition government came to power, (2010-2015) Michael Gove disagreed with, and disbands the Every Child Matters agenda, (Labour Left, 2012). Regardless of such, the significance of this theory remains, and is used by many. As noted aforesaid, within the UK, we have various policies in place, have carried out some research, and have relied on the US for understanding, and addressing the issues of gun's, gang's, delinquent behaviour, and the driving force behind such behaviours. However, to what lengths have we gone, to address the issues with those at the heart of the matter in order to establish policies that works? Part of our role as carer's/professionals is to listen and act upon information given to us. Moreover, do the policy makers and those who implement the given policies bother to 'listen' in order to hear what is been communicated which would empower them to compile policies and procedures which go some way to addressing the foresaid issues. These ostracised young people, may agree that they do not have a voice, within this condescending society. Furthermore, it may be appropriate to conclude that the numbers of young people in the secure estate, the size of the criminal justice budget as highlighted by Chris Grayling, and the very fact that gangs are still as prevalent today as they were fifteen years ago, is an indication that to a degree, the given policies are ineffective.

Working with victims and offenders

As you begin this section of this book there are some questions you may want to ask yourself about young offenders such as;

> When you think about victims and offenders who are they, what are their make-up?

> What is their his-tory? How does it make you feel?

> What's your feelings and views about the level of youth crime for example gangs and guns and social disorder?

> Is the penal system as it relates to young people working or should we be looking more to a system that focuses on help and education?

> What is your role when dealing with young offenders?

> Do you have the knowledge, experience and support to do your job successfully?

These are very important questions which you need to address in order to deal with transference of feelings emotions and personal views which will arise.

Within the social work training and professions, it is important to explore what we know about young people who come into the youth justice system, and may end up incarcerated. It is equally important to look at the responsibilities of the social work practitioner and how they can address some oppressive and inequitable factors that influence the lives of young offenders. When we look at the child welfare and the Youth Justice Systems, it gives the impression that they take unconnected approaches in addressing the needs of young people and signifies lack of joint up working. This view is to some extent reinforced by the way each system has differing aims and objectives when engaging with this groups and its concentrated interventions. As we are aware, to a greater extent social workers will always take a welfare-orientated approach, which will seeks to engage with vulnerable groups and individuals who come to the attention of the welfare system. On the other hand the youth justice system will be focused on interventions with convicted offenders which seek to rehabilitate and reduce crime, however neither are as cut and clear as they may sound. The separation of focused outcomes is further alienated, with responsibility of the youth justice system been placed under the control of the Ministry of Justice whilst the local authority social services department are responsible for the welfare system. Notwithstanding the very clear division in responsibilities, and how services are focused, it is also the case that victims and offenders are seen as being at opposing ends of the crime spectrum; with one end being the recipient of a felonious act and the other end the perpetrator of the action.

It has become the norm that when we think of victim and perpetrator a number of assumptions will automatically be concomitant, for example, in the first instance the victim will be perceived as helpless and with offender will be seen as violent and aggressive. However, not all incidences will be cut clear, as many young people will inhabit the role of victim and perpetrator equally. Consequently, social workers need to have a comprehensive understanding about young people who come into contact with the youth justice system in order to have a balanced view, which is based on data and research, and not on the influence of the media. Equally is an appreciation that these children and young people have a right to have their welfare safeguarded.

The function of the Children Act (CA) (1989) (2004) and (2014) is to safeguard and protect the welfare of children. The Children Act and any successive policy and procedures place an obligation on Social Service Departments to provide a service for children believed to be 'in need' or those who may need 'protection' consequently it deems the child's welfare as paramount importance. Local authorities have a duty to safe guard the welfare of all children in their area. However, this does not mean taking a heavy handed approach, and where possible the local authority must seek to permit children and young people to reside with their families, and working in partnership with parents and families to achieve this outcome (Children Act 1989). Further, to this the CA places other duties on local authorities which include assessments of children in need, and the provision of further support services where necessary. With the introduction of the Children Act, (2004) came the need for improved partnership working and the monitoring of outcomes between agencies. As noted earlier it also introduced the Every Child Matters agenda, that identified five positive outcomes for children and young people which were to; be healthy; stay safe; enjoy and achieve; make a positive contribution; and achieve economic well-being (Children Act 2004). On these premise it would denote that the every Child Matters agenda was welfare driven.

The principal aim of the youth justice service, is to prevent offending and reoffending by children and young people under the age of 18. The secure estate is supposed to be a safe environment, which facilitates the communication between staff and the young people, around the causes of their offending behaviour'. However how safe and conducive to the needs of these young people, the penal system has been is questionable. Between 1990 and 2014, a significant number of children and young people (age 24 and under) have died in custody, as was highlighted by the House of Commons Justice Committee (2012-13). Godson and Coles, (2008) identified that there has been in excess of 30 child deaths in prison.

INQUEST (2014.) published a breakdown of deaths of young people (aged 21 and under) in prisons and Young Offender Institutions (YOIs) by year since 1990. These findings were agreed by a House of Commons Justice Committee 2012-13 report (Google Books, 2013)

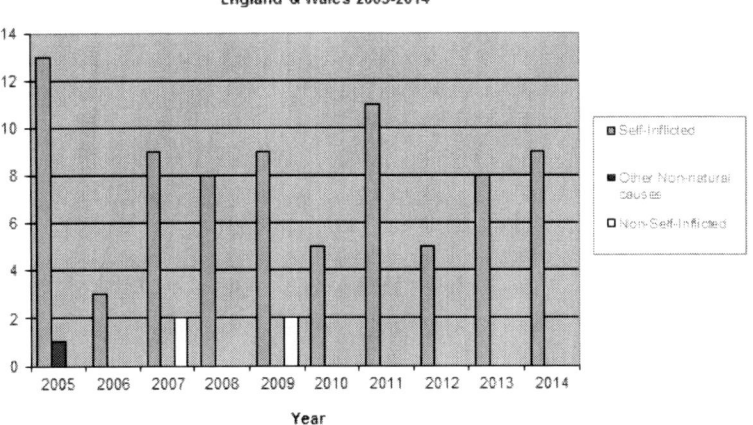

Fig. 1: Youth Deaths (21 and under) in Prison
England & Wales 2005-2014

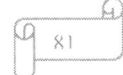

Below is a breakdown of deaths of young people (**aged 21 and under**) in prisons and Young Offender Institutions (YOIs) by year since 1990 (information sourced form INQUEST, 2014)

Table 1: Deaths of young people aged 21 and under in prison (England & Wales) 1990-date

Year	Self-Inflicted	Non-Self-Inflicted	Other Non-natural causes	Homicide	Awaiting Classification	Total
2015	1	1	0	0	1	3
2014	9	0	0	0	0	9
2013	8	0	0	0	0	8
2012	5	0	0	0	0	5
2011	11	0	0	0	0	11
2010	5	0	0	0	0	5
2009	9	2	0	0	0	11
2008	8	0	0	0	0	8
2007	9	2	0	0	0	11
2006	3	0	0	0	0	3
2005	13	0	1	0	0	14
2004	6	0	1	0	0	7
2003	13	2	0	0	0	15
2002	16	2	0	0	0	18
2001	15	0	0	0	0	15
2000	18	0	0	2	0	20
1999	19	1	0	0	0	20
1998	15	3	0	1	0	19
1997	16	1	0	2	0	19
1996	14	3	0	0	0	17
1995	11	0	0	1	0	12
1994	12	2	0	0	0	14
1993	3	0	0	0	0	3
1992	10	0	0	0	0	10
1991	5	0	0	0	0	5
1990	10	0	0	0	0	10
Total	264	19	2	6	1	292

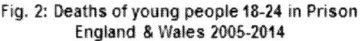

Fig. 2: Deaths of young people 18-24 in Prison
England & Wales 2005-2014

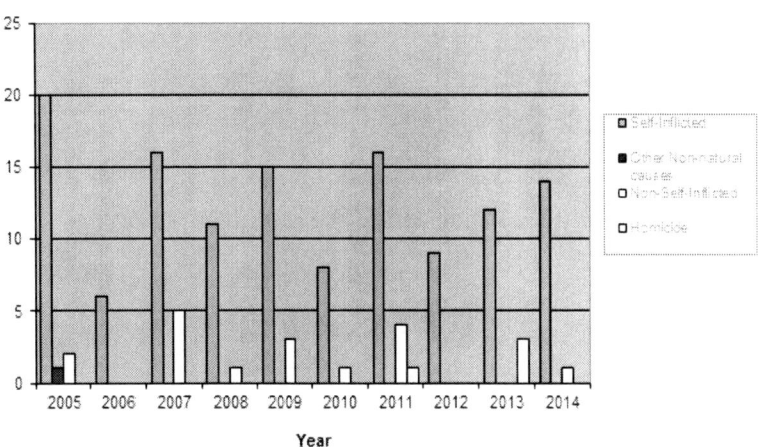

Below is a breakdown of deaths of young people aged 18-24 in prisons and Young Offender Institutions (YOIs) by year since 1990. (INQUEST 2014.)

Table 2: Deaths of young people aged 18-24 in prison (England & Wales) 1990-date

Year	Self-Inflicted	Non-Self-Inflicted	Other Non-natural causes	Homicide	Awaiting Classification	Total
2015	9	1	0	0	0	10
2014	15	2	0	0	3	20
2013	12	0	0	3	0	15
2012	9	0	0	0	0	9
2011	16	4	0	1	0	21
2010	8	1	0	0	0	9
2009	15	3	0	0	0	18
2008	11	1	0	0	0	12
2007	16	5	0	0	0	21
2006	6	0	0	0	0	6
2005	20	2	1	0	0	23

2004	18	3	1	0	0	22
2003	27	4	0	0	0	31
2002	24	3	0	0	0	27
2001	19	4	0	0	0	23
2000	25	0	0	2	0	27
1999	26	3	0	0	0	29
1998	20	6	0	1	0	27
1997	23	2	0	2	0	27
1996	14	3	0	0	0	17
1995	18	1	0	1	0	20
1994	17	3	0	0	0	20
1993	6	0	0	0	0	6
1992	10	0	0	0	0	10
1991	4	0	0	0	0	4
1990	11	0	0	0	0	11
Total	406	52	2	10	3	473

Notwithstanding the astounding revelation of these figures it was noted by INQUEST (2014) that "deaths of young people that occurred in Secure Training Centres (STCs) do not appear in these figures as STCs are in the custody of the Youth Justice Board rather than the Prison Service".

INQUEST further argued that systemic neglect, institutional complacency and short-sighted policies have contributed to the deaths of children and young people. Notwithstanding this, one can conclude that these deaths are the most extreme outcome, of a system that continues to fail some of society's most disadvantaged children, young people and families.

It can be further argued that the number of deaths in prison is high, due to the fact it is overused as a societal solution, to a range of social problems that should be addressed elsewhere. Many young people are systematically failed by the education services, as well as other social and welfare services well before they entered the Prison

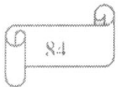

system, an ineffective and expensive intervention that doesn't work as highlighted earlier by the high recidivism rates. INQUEST (2014) further highlighted that a succeeding report, Stolen Lives and Missed Opportunities continued previous research, by collating evidence about the deaths of 65 children and young people in prison between 2011 and 2014. Drawing on a unique data they were able to elucidate the extreme vulnerabilities of these groups – "many which were care leavers and suffering from acute mental health issues, early life trauma and special educational needs". These are young people who should have been wrapped around by the various Children Act which is aimed at protecting and safeguarding the welfare of children and young people.

Irrespective of the aforesaid, (high crime rates, youth dearth in custody etc.) The youth justice board has what can be seen as a disproportionate number of legislation relating to children and young people who commit criminal acts which are inclusive of Crime and Disorder Act 1998; Youth Justice and Criminal Evidence Act 1999; Criminal Justice Act 2003; Anti-Social Behaviour Act 2003; Criminal Justice and Immigration Act 2008. In line with the Crime and Disorder Act 1998 the Youth Offending Teams were created. There is a YOT in every local authority in England and Wales which is made up of a multidisciplinary team made up of representatives from the housing, health and social services, police, probation, education, drugs and alcohol misuse.

The role of the YOT is to identify the challenging areas of a young person's life (10–18 years of age) that may be a causal factor in their offending behaviour. This is done by way of an assessment, using a national assessment tool called 'Asset'. This assessment tool is used to highlights specific areas of concern relating to offending behaviour, thus enabling the YOT practitioner to identify appropriate programmes aimed at addressing these issues with a long term intention of preventing further offending.

Consecutive governments regardless of their political affiliation have experimented with a range of approaches in addressing crime in the UK. In recent years we have had the Labour Government policy 'tough on crime, tough on the causes of crime', and the Conservative party who hold the monopoly on punitive approaches as a means of addressing the issues of persistent criminal activities, particularly the activities of our youth. England and Wales still have the highest detention rates for young people in Europe, (Muncie 2009, qtd at Fox and Arnull, 2013) second only to Turkey, (Youth Crime in England and Wales, n.d.). Goldson, (2006, p5) discusses the fact that the high numbers of incarceration has been "linked to numerous factors relating to legislation and policy implementation", and attitudes "where youth crime is deemed insufferable and must be dealt with severely". This lead to the question of what is the views on youth offending by other countries and are their good practices and lessons to be learnt.

It is irrefutable that a key component that runs through the lives of a vast amount of young people involved in criminal activates is that of poverty. This is confirmed by Goldson and Muncie, (Goldson and Muncie, 2006, 2008: 222), who maintain that the 'corollaries between child poverty, social and economic inequality, youth crime and criminalisation are undeniable'. Poverty has been identified as a defining feature of many social service users and a perpetual social issue that the social work profession has done little to address or change by Fox and Arnull, 2013

Poverty, education and environment have all been seen as contributing factors to youth delinquency. Coupled with the aforesaid are issue associated with mental issues.

Hagell, 2002; Arnull et al, (2005 p 5) argued that young people in the youth justice system were three times more likely to have mental health needs than that of their peers. These findings were further verified by Lader et al. (2000 qtd by Fox and Arnull, 2013 p, 8), who noted that "eight out of ten young people in custody met the criteria for more than one formal mental health diagnosis.

Notwithstanding the fact that BME are more frequently excluded from the education system than their peers, it is well documented that young people, especially males from Black and Minority Ethnic (BME) groups, are over represented within the youth justice system (Páll Sveinsson, 2012). Furthermore, although studies don't seem to show why, it is the case that this group will often receive harsher sentences then their peers, consequently there is a larger number of BME in the prison population (House of Commons Home Affairs Committee, 2007), and the recidivism numbers remain ever concerning.

It is acknowledged that the deficiency in statutory education is one of the fundamental factors linked to recidivism (Youth Justice Board, 2005). Given the acceptance of the positive role education has in reducing offending and reoffending rates, the Government's lack of commitment in imposing legislation that guarantees local authorities are responsible for the education provision for young offenders in custody settings is of great concern (Children and Young People Now 2011 qtd by Fox and Arnull, 2013 p, 8).

The concerns about young people in the youth justice system in the lack of education during rehabilitation was corroborated by Chris Grayling, the justice secretary who acknowledged that there needs to be 'change within the secure estate. In the green paper on the future of youth custody, he speaks about "putting education at the heart of detention" for the 1,500 young offenders currently held in

YOIs, local authority secure units and privately run secure training centres' across England and Wales (ITV News, 2013, Travis, 2013). Grayling further argued that "the youth custody green paper would provide` an opportunity for a radically different approach": he highlighted that "Some youth custodial places cost £200,000, five times the cost of sending a child to a top private school". Notwithstanding this "nearly three-quarters of young people leaving custody re-offend" within a very short time of release. Grayling argued, "It is irresponsible of us to keep pouring money into a system that doesn't work in the hope of a different outcome". He further commented that this didn't make sense to the taxpayer or to the young people who we should be trying to get back on the straight and narrow." Mr Grayling was of the view that we needed a fresh look at how we rehabilitated young people who commit crime. He thought that we should "have secure training colleges which provide education in a period of detention rather than detention with education as an afterthought". (Travis 2013)

In reality social works practicing in a youth justice team, inclusive of the prison settings is different from practicing in a more traditional social work setting. Children who come into contact with the welfare system will range from birth to 18. This age rang maybe extended depending of the individual child, for example if they are in education. Those in the youth justice system will range from 10 to 18 years. The range of children and young people in the YJS will consistently be that of children and young people who have been convicted of, or are accused of committing a crime. This area of practice may be unfamiliar for many practitioners as the tendency for social work practitioners is to practice within children services (looked after children, children in need or even fostering and adoption) what is also unhelpful is the lack of literature regarding social work with offenders, gang or this age group.

In order to expedite your practice and empower your interaction with this service user group it maybe in one's the best interest to develop a comprehensive view of this group, what makes them tick, who is a victim and who is a perpetrator? In order to fulfil your obligation to this group, you will have to move away from the traditional thinking, and the theories of these young people, that have been conveyed by the media. By moving away from the out-of-date notion of someone who has experienced crime in the eyes of the law, to one that encompasses a wide-ranging definition in terms of lifestyle and limited choices, you begin to have a more comprehensive understanding of who these children and young people are. Having a broader view and understanding of this group should in no way diminish your views on the devastating effects of their criminal activities', or the victim impact. Notwithstanding this and of equal importance one needs to have an appreciation that many of the young people with whom you will come into contact with, within the youth justice system will be both victims and offenders interchangeably. Therefore, it is important for you to have an in-depth understanding of this context, which will assist with your knowledge and the way in which you approach young people. Working with this group will also require you to have an understanding of the personal and structural oppression and discrimination affecting the lives of many young people who offend. Further, to this there are a number of identified social, biological, structural and legal factors including poverty, gender, offending peer group, family (including inadequate supervision), offending family members, lack of education, abuse, loss, fetal alcohol syndrome, post-traumatic stress disorder or other brain trauma, mental health difficulties, stress, anxiety, depression, alcohol and substance misuse that maybe prevalent to varying degrees in the lives of young people who commit criminal acts (Cormack, 1996 Feilzer and Hood, 2004; Smith, 2006; Arnull and Eagle, 2009, cited by Fox and Arnull, 2013 p, 9)

The evidence that relates to the lack of educational provision in custody is somewhat concerning, this coupled with the disproportionate number of young males from black minority ethnic groups incarcerated highlights a major ethical concern not just for the ruling party (Conservative) but more so, for service providers e.g. Social work practitioners due to the lack of autonomy, equality and positive outcomes. Given the value base and ethical nature of social work practice, these concerns will resonate with the traditional aims of social work and its ethos of empowerment regarding particular marginalized groups and individuals

Outnumbered and out powered are they winning the war?

Although the behaviour of young people who commit crime can be alarming, these young people do not live a life without value or ethic as is often portrayed by society. These young people are often ones who were brought up in the church and have morals and social values which at the time of their offences seem far removed. However these young people seem to believe they are fighting their own war which often leads them to dismiss or forget the social and moral values instilled.

Is it the case that the government is outnumbered, and out powered by the incidence of youth crime, and if so what are the consequences of this?

Over the years we have seen the numbers of youth gangs grow vastly in numbers. The impact of this has meant more incidences of youth deaths, destroyed families and a rise of youth incarceration. Additionally, the financial encumbrances on taxpayers has been a criminal offense within itself. Chris Grayling youth custody green paper acknowledged that "Some youth custodial places cost £200,000, five times the cost of sending a child to a top private school" (Travis, 2013) Relentlessly and regardless of Mr Grayling's conclusions (Putting education at the heart of detention) the punitive system remains the same, and the provisions within the secure estate remaining contemptible. It was noted by the justice secretary Chris Grayling that "education in youth custody is currently provided on contract by a range of institutions including further education colleges. One of the main providers, Manchester College, has been criticized in recent years for the poor quality of its courses provided at the YOIs", however nothing has changed thus evidencing a lack of commitment to improve on youth rehabilitation. Notwithstanding the lack of education and commitment to positive rehabilitation, it has been long argued that custody is a breeding ground for further crime. With countless hours to pass and the lack of education, exercise or constructive pastime those incarcerated will often pass time with conversation. Samenow, Ph.D, (2011) argued that "the main topics of conversations in prison generally concern crime, drugs, and gossip about who will do what and to whom". He further explained, some commit crimes while incarcerated, and plan new crimes that they will commit once they are released. What is more concerning is the fact that some of these youth are so well connected, and held in high esteem that they are able to engineer crimes that, upon their say so, will be commit in the community. These young men are known as "shot callers" or gang leaders, who have the influence to reaches beyond prison walls (Samenow, Ph.D, 2011). If these findings, coupled with others are to be taken literally, it may indicate that the government are losing the war on youth crime. However, the government will not be discouraged by their methodology.

Trident metropolitan unit dedicated to black on black crime

During the late 90's it was suggested that shootings were disproportionately affecting black communities (Webbe, 2013). These violent crimes were proving hard to investigate due to lack of trust and confidence in the police and witness fear of reprisals.

Wider support for a dedicated unit to tackle gun crime grew from June 1998 following the separate murders of two black women; Avril Johnson in Briton and Michelle Carby in Stratford. Following the Lawrence Inquiry 1999, agreement was reached for the establishment of a dedicated operational command unit and in June 2000 the Operation Trident OCU was launched, (Webbe, 2013) and worked closely with the Operation Trident Independent Advisory Group (IAG). During its early days Lee Jasper, who was chief race advisor to London mayor, argued that "the police and communities could not compete with the resources of drug gangs in the effort to keep disillusioned young black men away from crime". He further noted that with London's crack economy now worth an estimated £500m, government needed to pour money into community activism if they were going to stand a chance of turning back gun and drug-related crime in the most deprived areas" (Casciani, 2003). Notwithstanding the fact that gun men were attacking each other in turf wars, the police were also targeted. During Christmas 2006 one of Britain's longest sieges took place in Hackney East London. The gun man who had a string of convictions and had been to prison on several occasions, shot at police on several occasions after he had barricaded himself into a building where he died 15 days later (Cowan, 2005). Irrespective of the inferences made by Mr Jasper Trident continued to fight against black on black crime and developed a relationship with the community.

It is suggested by the Met Police that "over the years the nature of shootings in London has changed" (Police, 2015). They further note that "ten years ago, those responsible for shootings were mainly organized criminals from Jamaica, however in recent years the victims and perpetrators of shootings are from all backgrounds" (Police, 2015). The Met further argued "there has also been a significant increase in the proportion of younger males involved in shootings; about two thirds of shooting victims are aged under 24 years old. Motivations for offending have also changed and approximately 50% of shootings involve individuals connected to gangs" (Police, 2015).

In February 2012, the MPS launched the new Trident Gang Crime Command, expanding their remit of Trident from its previous focus on shootings to proactively tackling wider gang crime. Trident now has additional resources, including Operation Connect, to develop a coordinated police response to gang crime, whilst working with partners to divert young people away from gangs.

Communication personal Space and boundaries.

As adults, parents but more so and service providers, we play a big part in diverting young people from serious crime and offending. In order to do so we need to be able to engage with them. However, communication seems to be an area that we struggle, and requires us to address the following question:

Why do we as adults often find it hard to communicate with young people?

Why do we often feel like young people are speaking a different language?

Is good communication inclusive of good boundaries?

How do we establish good communication?

Why as adult and people in authority do we feel we know best and are reluctant to listen, in order to hear what young people are saying?

As professionals and parents we often listen to respond, and do not necessarily 'hear' what has been communicated by young people

Is it the case that preconceived views can have an impact on one ability to fully engage and provide a 'good enough' service?

Interpersonal skills

As part of a human race interpersonal skills are the life skills we use every day to communicate and interact with other people, both individually and in groups. People who have worked on developing strong interpersonal skills are usually more successful in both their professional and personal lives. However interpersonal skill are not necessarily one of the skill which are listed as essential when applying for the role of a social worker. This deficiency may contribute to the difficulties that some social workers and other professionals often in communicating with the service users, especially young people.

Our Interpersonal Skills are Inclusive of the following:

Verbal Communication - What we say and how we say it.

Non-Verbal Communication - What we communicate without words, body language is an example.

Listening Skills - How we interpret both the verbal and non-verbal messages sent by others.

Negotiation - Working with others to find a mutually agreeable outcome.

Problem Solving - Working with others to identify, define and solve problems.

Decision Making – Exploring and analysing options to make sound decisions.

Assertiveness – Communicating our values, ideas, beliefs, opinions, needs and wants freely.

The next heading aim to help you think about the importance of verbal communicate, the processes involved and how to ensure that verbal or spoken messages are received as intended reducing any misunderstandings and miscommunication.

Verbal Communication

Effective verbal communication is reliant on a number of factors which cannot be isolated from other interpersonal skills such as non-verbal communication, listening skills and clarification. We will agree that in many interpersonal encounters, the first few minutes are exceptionally important as first impressions 'count' and has significant impact on the success of further communication. Moreover, the first few minutes can be very arduous when meeting with service users (young people and or resistant families) who are reluctant to work with services. Aside from this, you may be further disadvantaged, if you have no understanding of their story or demographic of the given area. What's more, everyone including the young people will have expectations as to how they want the meeting to proceed, and rightly or wrongly people tend to behave according to these expectations. If these expectations are far removed from each other, communication will not be effective or run smoothly. Consequently a starting point is to be fully equipped with the history and challenges of the community and the young people who exists within it. Been adequately informed, will support your clarity of speech, without been patronising. Retaining a calm and focused disposition, being polite and following some basic rules of etiquette will all aid the process of verbal communication, and open the door to dialog with a resistant service user. At a first meeting, formalities and appropriate greetings are usually expected: such formalities could include a handshake, an introduction to yourself, eye contact and discussion around a neutral subject such as their well-being may be useful. A friendly disposition and smiling face are much more likely to encourage communication, than a blank face which may indicate preconceived views and judgments, thus there is a need to always be mindful of your body language and what it is saying. Nevertheless challenges may arise when using verbal communication, such as misunderstandings due to poor choice of words. It is equally important to have an understanding of language barriers. Subjective opinions regarding acceptable language may also have an impact and result in communication difficulties.

Language barriers are a major cause of confusion when communicating verbally. According to the University of Louisville, differences in language influenced by geographic location, education and social status can create barriers even among those who speak the same language (Hanes 2015)

Reinforcement

A publication by Skills You Need, highlighted that "the use of encouraging words alongside non-verbal gestures such as head nods, a warm facial expression and maintaining eye contact, are more likely to reinforce openness in others" (Skillsyouneed.com, 2015)

It may be agreed that it is often hard to engage with young people who are resistant to authority and professionals. However, the use of encouragement and positive reinforcement when interacting with this group, can begin to break down barriers and; signify an interest in what they have to say, thus paving the way for development and/or maintenance of a relationship

Effective Listening

The skills of Active Listening, 'Clarification and Reflection' may help with the young people you engage with. However, as noted above there can be barriers to effective communication, and a skilled communicator (social worker) also needs to be aware of effective communication and how to avoid or overcome these barriers in order to develop a working relationship with young people who are often labelled as "hard to engage"

There are many barriers to communication and these may occur at any stage from your first meeting or during an established working relationship. Barriers may lead to your message becoming distorted and you therefore risk wasting both time and resources by causing confusion and misunderstanding between you and the young person. Effective communication involves overcoming these barriers and conveying a clear and concise message

In every area of life 'Active listening' is a significant skill and yet, as communicators, people spend too much energy considering what they are going to say, rather than listening to what is being said. As a result, we listen to respond and not to hear what is actually being communicated. This position often causes discontent in the working relationship with young people.

In working with a young person we should always be prepared. In order to prepare oneself to actively listen we should ensure that the environment is conducive to the purpose of the meeting, for example where possible a warm and light room with minimal background noise or interruption.

Been prepared to listen and participate in a meeting means we are not thinking about our own personal stuff or the report we still have to prepare. We need to have an open mind in order to concentrate on the speaker's message. Having an open mind means one should avoid trying to think of your next question while the other person is giving information, you may be surprised that a lot of your questions are addressed in their conversation.

Have an unbiased mind-set

It is important to avoid making judgement. The very core of your training, taught you not to have a judgemental attitude, thus always have an open mind as things are not always what they seem, for example victims are perpetrators and vice versa.

The speaker (young person or family member) should not be stereotyped. Try not to let prejudices associated with, gender, ethnicity, social class, appearance, dress, association, involvement in the criminal justice system impact what is being communicated, as general

communication without any barriers, can reveal a lot of information without direct questioning.

Notwithstanding the aforesaid, there will need to be a certain amount of questioning. Effective questioning which is ethical, is an essential skill which should possessed be by all social workers. In spite of the aforementioned, social workers need to bear in mind that they are 'social workers' and not the police and consequently questioning should be done with some degree of empathy. Questioning which is conducted in a conversational way can be used to:

Begin a conversation.

Show interest in a person you are engaging with.

Acquire information.

Seek agreement for information sharing, further work to be undertaken, or even for the service user to agree to engage with services.

During all meetings and conversations, it is important to assess one's understanding of the information being shared, this can be done in a conversational manner

During a meaningful conversation it is possible to use both open and closed Questions.

As we are aware open questions will increase the scope for response, as they demand additional discussion and elaboration. For example, "How have you been since?" or "Can you please tell me more about….?" Open questions will take longer to answer, but they will give the young person far more scope for self-expression and encourage involvement in the conversation. However the rules of engagement for open questioning, will not always apply as young people my still answer an open question as though it were a closed question for example "how have you been"? OK. Can you please tell me more about? Nope. Why are you not able to tell me more about…….? "Because I don't want to". This for them is often their code of silence or loyalty. Consequently, your open question are often turned into closed questions thus providing only a one or two word answers (often simply 'yes', 'no' or maybe) and, in doing, limits the scope of fluent conversation. Two examples of closed questions are "Did you travel by bus today?" and "What football team do you support?" Questions of this kind means control of the communication is maintained by the social worker. However, this is not a desired outcome when trying to encourage the participation of others in a conversation. Nevertheless, closed questions can be beneficial for focusing discussion and obtaining clear, concise answers when needed.

Reflecting and Clarifying

As social workers we are taught the importance of reflective practice. Reflecting, is the process of feeding-back to another person your understanding of what has been said.

The key principle in using reflective skills involves identifying the person's core message and offering it back to them in your own words.

The practice of reflecting involves paraphrasing the message, capturing the essence of the facts and feelings expressed, and communicating your understanding back to the young person. In so doing you can check:

That you have understood what they have said.

The young person gets feedback as to how, you have understood what they told you.

Further to the above, you show interest in, and respect for, what the young person has said. You are also demonstrating to the young person that you are able to consider their viewpoint.

When communicating with young people Non-Verbal Communication is just as important as verbal communication and sometimes can be even more important if you know what to look for, thus applying critical observation to presentation etc.

Non-verbal communications are inclusive of facial expressions, the tone and pitch of the voice, and body language. These non-verbal signals can give clues and additional information and meaning over and above spoken communication.

Within today's society young people's allegiances will often be displayed by the colours that the wear. This non-verbal communication can provided you with some information on which to base your verbal communication.

Interpersonal communication does not only involve the explicit meaning of words, the information or message conveyed, but also refers to implicit messages, whether intentional or not, which are expressed through non-verbal behaviours.(Skills You Need 2015)

Barriers to effective communication

Verbal or non-verbal communication can be difficult if there are barriers. There are many reasons why interpersonal communications may fail. Due to reasons unintended, the message which is being conveyed may not be received exactly the way the young person intended. For this reason, it is therefore important, that the social worker seeks feedback, to check that the message/information which they are receiving, is what is being conveyed. There are numerous barriers to effective communication (Interpersonal skills ToolClicks, n.d.). However, within social work as it relates to young people, namely those in the criminal justice, this list can be reduced to Psychological barriers and attitudinal barriers

Psychological Barriers

The psychological state of the communicators (young person) will influence how messages are sent, received and perceived. Young people, you will come into contact with, will often have various things going on for example, criminal justice issues, family issues peer issues to name a few. These issues coupled with stress and anger will often contribute to ineffective communication. The young people social workers come into contact with, are often angry for one reason or another. Anger is another example of a psychological barrier to communication. However, the level of anger exhibited at any given time will differ, for that reason, there is no room for preconceived views. Furthermore it goes without saying that every young person should be treated as an individual regardless of their history and or affiliations. Further to this, it is equally important that the given worker takes a humane viewpoint when conversing with these young people as, when we are angry it is easy to say things, that we may later regret and also to misconstrue what others are saying.

By the same token, it is important to remember and acknowledge that, very often the face that these young people are showing is a façade, and they are very often, individuals with low confidence and self-esteem when removed from the protection of their peers. With this in mind it is then worth noting that generally people with low self-esteem may be less assertive and therefore may not feel comfortable communicating - they may feel shy about saying how they really feel or read negative sub-texts into the messages they hear. They will also be mistrusting of services and people in authority, for example the police, court system, prisons and social workers. These are all entities known as 'the system'.

Attitudinal Barriers

Root, (2015) argued that attitudes are commonly formed by an individual's opinions or personal feelings on a subject or person and can be difficult to alter

Attitudinal barriers are behaviours or perceptions that prevent people from communicating effectively. The young people within the criminal justice system and even the care system to some degree may display attitudinal barriers. Attitudinal barriers to communication may affect the individuals taking part in a conversation. This barrier may be a result of personality conflicts, a lack of motivation and or a mistrust of people and service providers. As professionals we will all deny having preconceived ideas or attitudinal barriers. However, to say you never experience any of the above will be an ethical issue in itself. Consequently, the receivers of messages (social worker) should attempt to overcome their own attitudinal barriers and preconceived views in order to successfully facilitate effective communication. This in turn may encourage the young person with whom one is engaging in conversation, to do the same.

Summarising and Closing Communication is equally as important, as the introduction and main communication

A summary of a conversation is an overview of the main points or issues discussed. Summarising can also serve the same purpose as 'reflecting' which is an important process for social workers. More importantly, summarising allows both parties to examine and agree the information exchanged between them. When used effectively, summarising should also serve as a guide to any further actions needed. Having covered all points and

summarised your conversation, you come to the point of closure.

The way conversations are closed or ended will form a significant part of the working relationship and goes a long way to determining the way our conversation is remembered. Consequently, closing a conversation/discussion abruptly will not allow the other person to 'round off' what they are saying, thus you should ensure there is time for controlled closure allowing the young person to have some control. In order to bring a conversation-meeting to a positive close you can use a range of gentle signs, such as telling them you know they have been here for a while, closing notepads-books and asking what they have planned for the rest of the day. The closure of your conversation is a good time to make any future arrangements and agree any follow-up appointments.

A child-centred approach

As a social worker you will be aware that safeguarding systems ensure that the welfare of the child is paramount (Workingtogetheronline.co.uk, 2015) The failure of a safeguarding systems may result in losing sight of the needs and views of the child/ren within the system, or even placing the interests of adults ahead of the needs of children, this may be the need or views of the service provider, for example cooperate parenting. It is the case that the children and young people we work with, are clear about what they want from an effective safeguarding system, which is as follows:

They want to be respected, and their views heard, to have stable consistent relationships with professionals, built on trust and to have reliable support provided. The views of the service user, (children and young people) should guide the performance of professionals. All social care professionals working with children should see and

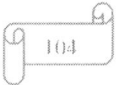

speak to the child with the same courtesy that they require from them; listen to what they say; take their views seriously; and work with them collectively when deciding how to support their needs. If a 10 year old can be charged with murder, and held responsible for their actions, the same principle should apply when working with children, you are providing a service to; for example they should be old enough to have a view and make a coherent decision. As discussed above the Children Act 1989 dictates that the welfare of children be safe guarded. Moreover this Act requires local authorities to have due regard to a child's wishes when deciding what services it will provide under section 17 of the Children Act 1989, and before making any decisions about action to be taken to protect individual children under section 47 of the Children Act 1989. These duties complement the requirements relating to the wishes and feelings of children who are, or may be, looked after (section 22(4) Children Act 1989), including those who are provided with accommodation under section 20 of the Children Act 1989 and children taken into police protection (section 46(3)(d) of that Act). Further to this is the Equality Act 2010 which puts a further responsibility on public authorities, inclusive of social services, health etc. to eradicate discrimination and promote equality of opportunity. It is an Assumption of the Act that no child or group of children should be treated less favourably than others in being able to access effective services which meet their individual needs. However children and young people who experience marginalisation (exclusion from school, deprivation, the criminal justice system) even care leavers, often find it difficult to access the required services. Subsequently removing themselves from the norms of requiring any support thereof service providers who fail them in so many ways.

Conclusion

The research of this book relied substantially on electronic data, which is both deep-rooted and conversant 'with' relevant knowledge information to support ones study and practice.

Highlighted above and supported by research, are many contributing factors to the rise of delinquent and violent behaviour amongst our youth. It would be inappropriate to say that any one factor, plays a more prominent role than the other. However, what is true to say, and highlighted by a Home Office document, is crime involving firearms was up 55% in 2004/05 compared to the previous year, and there seems to be no tangible data to contradict these findings or show a reduction to date . It is clear that the raise of violent behaviour amongst the youth has helped to shape many policies, aimed at addressing these issues, as well as impacting on the changing role of the social workers. In the past instead of the juvenile system been welfare focused, it was focused on punishment regardless of the presenting issues, thus crime before welfare. However, more recently in an attempt to address welfare matters, as highlighted above, in association youth offending workers, we have seen the involvement of social workers in the youth justice system. The introduction of Every Child Matters and Changes for Children could have helped to address some of the issues and concerns raised above. However, with the Coalition Government (2010-2015) the outlook for children changed substantially, with deeper deprivation, social exclusion and those involved in anti-social youth groups (gangs) getting younger. Moreover, what seems to be clear is there are no signs of the welfare of children who live in poverty and deprivation changing in the near future without substantial and focused intervention. Furthermore it seems the coined phase of the "gang", has been a sufficient explanation for the root causes of the youth ills, and no other attempts have been made to understand the wide-ranging and complex social,

cultural, economic and political context of youth violence. The punitive, dogmatic system, and the criminalising of children which is used by the government to address the ill which may be born out of deprivation is clearly not working. Consequently, it can be asked, how long will it take the 'powers that be' to acknowledge the inadequate systems, for example education, the court process and prison, as well as the inability of many local authorities to provide a person centred approach to the families who need it most.

We have seen many years of youth deprivation, unemployment, criminality and social exclusion. We have seen the social norms dictated by those in power challenged by discontented youth, as seen by the London Riots 2010 (Beckford, 2012) which creates disharmony within society further ostracising these young people, we are trying to bring back into the realms of the given 'social norms'. With every passing day, week month and year that these unacceptable anomalies persist (social depravation, social exclusion, class division, to name a few) it will become harder to rebalance the norms of society. In order to rebuild a moral disposition of todays' youth, who are tomorrows' future, the government will have to stop the lip service, stop making it part of their manifesto to address crime (which never has much impact after an election) and get up and attack crime from its root causes. It is reprehensible for a government department (who can also be termed as a gang) to find it acceptable that continuing generations live in poverty, (through no fault of their own thus excluding generational benefit claimers) deprivation on the same scale as a third world country, where the youth associated behaviour (gang crimes) is in direct correlation of that which they suffer, and the government continues to develop a punitive system, which has little impact on altering unwanted, unacceptable behaviour. Moreover, it is an ongoing crime that MP's, continue to be the fat cats of the land, never experiencing any of the issues outlined in this book e.g. depravation, debt, or social exclusion. They continue to cut benefits to the neediest, but award themselves benefits, and pay rises to support their standards of living they have carved out for themselves. Thereafter those in power who have attributed to these happenings, wonder why young people feel there is an injustice in this bigoted society in which equality does not exists, where the rich get richer and the poor get poorer, and they feel they will never be able to attain the standard of living afforded to those that already have. The way these young people feel maybe justified, however their actions are targeted at each other and innocent communities which cannot be justified. Accordingly, in order to reduce and eradicate these happenings, as professionals we need to be proactive and consistent in the service we deliver. Notwithstanding this, and as noted above the government needs to be held accountable for their actions. They will have to stop behaving in this bigoted fashion, and make good on the many manifestos, in relation to deprivation, education, youth unemployment and the rethinking of the youth justice system which puts them in the driving seat.

In order to rebuild a country which is Abundant, not only in wealth, but more so in social morals and social cohesion, a 'Great' amount of actions consistency and commitment is needed:

ARE YOU READY TO FACE THE CHALLENGE

We are "Taking Positive Steps" and Associates Ltd
Find us on Linkedin, Facebook, Twitter and Youtube

Reference

Abbott, D. (2002). *Diane Abbott: Teachers are failing black boys.* [online] the Guardian. Available at: http://www.theguardian.com/politics/2002/jan/06/pu blicservices.race [Accessed 23 Aug. 2007].

Afroeurope.blogspot.co.uk, (2013). *AFRO-EUROPE: The migration of Black people from the Caribbean to Europe.* [online] Available at: http://afroeurope.blogspot.co.uk/2013/06/the-migration-of-black-people-from.html [Accessed 7 Jul. 2014].

Aldridge, J. and Medina-Ariza, J. (2007). *Youth Gangs in an English City: Social Exclusion, Drugs and Violence: ESRC Research Summary, RES-000-23-0615. Swindon: ESRC.* [online] Esrc.ac.uk. Available at: http://www.esrc.ac.uk/my-esrc/grants/RES-000-23-0615/outputs/Read/1c3755d3-da13-4bcb-b87a-2973d2798d8b [Accessed 11 Aug. 2009].

Alexander, C. (2008). *(Re)thinking Gangs* [online] Available at: http://www.runnymedetrust.org/uploads/publications/pdfs/RethinkingGangs-2008.pdf [Accessed 23 Aug. 2011].

Anderson, A. (2007). *News - Latest breaking UK news.* [online] Telegraph.co.uk. Available at: http://www.telegraph.co.uk/news/main.jhtml?xml=/news/2007/08/12/ngang112.xml [Accessed 10 Feb. 2011].

Anderson-Dixon, C. (2013). *Has the medias creation of moral panics caused our society to decline?* [online] Western Eye. Available at: http://www.westerneye.net/comment/2013/02/has-the-medias-creation-of-moral-panics-caused-our-society-to-decline/ [Accessed 9 May 2014].

AOAV, (2014). *15 shootings that changed the law: Dunblane, 1996 | AOAV.* [online] Available at: https://aoav.org.uk/2014/dunblane-1996/ [Accessed

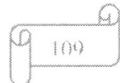

19 Nov. 2014].

Arthur, R. (2005). Punishing Parents for the Crimes of their Children. *Howard J*, 44(3), pp.233-253.

Arthur, R. (2012). Rethinking the Criminal Responsibility of Young People in England and Wales. *European Journal of Crime, Criminal Law and Criminal Justice*, 20(1), pp.13-29.

Atkinson, F. and Ubiribo, E. (n.d.). *Young People Guns Knives and Gangs.* [online] Csas.org.uk. Available at: http://www.csas.org.uk/upload/documents/webpage/ Conference%20III/YPeopleGKG.pdf. [Accessed 20 Jun. 2011].

Baaf.org.uk, (2014). *Update on BAAF project: alternatives to custody for young offenders | British Association for Adoption and Fostering.* [online] Available at: http://www.baaf.org.uk/media/releases/update-baaf-project-alternatives-custody-young-offenders [Accessed 18 Nov. 2014].

Barter, C. and Berridge, D. (2011). *Children behaving badly?* Chichester, West Sussex: Wiley-Blackwell.

Basw.co.uk, (2015). *Independent review: Keeping children in care out of trouble, Prison Reform Trust (2015) | BASW Resources.* [online] Available at: https://www.basw.co.uk/resource/?id=4119 [Accessed 19 Aug. 2015].

Batty, D. (2002). *Key figures in the Climbié case.* [online] the Guardian. Available at: http://www.theguardian.com/society/2002/feb/04/1 [Accessed 20 Oct. 2008].

Batty, D. (2010). *James Bulger's killers were old enough to face trial, insists government.* [online] the Guardian. Available at: http://www.theguardian.com/uk/2010/mar/13/bulger-jon-venables-maggie-atkinson [Accessed 19 Aug. 2011].

Bbc.co.uk, (2014). *BBC - GCSE Bitesize: Important*

reforms - summary. [online] Available at:
http://www.bbc.co.uk/schools/gcsebitesize/history/m
wh/britain/liberalreformsrev1.shtml [Accessed 19
Apr. 2015].

Beckford, M. (2012). *London riots: Almost 1,000 jailed as judges give tougher sentences.* [online]
Telegraph.co.uk. Available at:
http://www.telegraph.co.uk/news/uknews/crime/910
1436/London-riots-Almost-1000-jailed-as-judges-give-tougher-sentences.html [Accessed 11 Dec.
2013].

Biblegateway.com, (n.d.). *BibleGateway.com: A searchable online Bible in over 100 versions and 50 languages.* [online] Available at:
https://www.biblegateway.com [Accessed 13 Sep.
2013].

Bowcott, O., Ball, J. and Rogers, S. (2011). *Race variation in jail sentences, study suggests.* [online] the
Guardian. Available at:
http://www.theguardian.com/law/2011/nov/25/ethnic
-variations-jail-sentences-study [Accessed 7 Mar.
2012].

Briggs, S. (2015). *Important Theories in Criminology: Why People Commit Crime - For Dummies.* [online]
Dummies.com. Available at:
http://www.dummies.com/how-to/content/important-theories-in-criminology-why-people-commi.html
[Accessed 18 Aug. 2015].

Bulger, R. and Dunn, R. (n.d.). *My James.*

Camber, R. (2010). *Black men 'to blame for most violent city crime'... but they're also the victims.* [online]
Mail Online. Available at:
http://www.dailymail.co.uk/news/article-
1290047/Metropolitan-Police-crime-statistics-reveal-violent-criminals-black--victims.html [Accessed 20
May 2011].

Casciani, D. (2003). *BBC NEWS | UK | Gun crime 'threat'*

to UK minorities. [online] News.bbc.co.uk. Available at: http://news.bbc.co.uk/1/hi/uk/3035357.stm [Accessed 31 Aug. 2007].

Cesi.org.uk, (2015). *Child Poverty | Inclusion.* [online] Available at: http://cesi.org.uk/keypolicy/child-poverty [Accessed 19 Jul. 2015].

Chambliss, W., Mankoff, M., Pearce, F. and Snider,, L. (n.d.). *Traditional Marxist Perspectives on Crime.* [online] Sociology.org.uk. Available at: http://www.sociology.org.uk/pcdevmx.pdf. [Accessed 27 Jul. 2011].

Cherry, K. (n.d.). *The 4 Styles of Parenting.* [online] About.com Education. Available at: http://psychology.about.com/od/developmentalpsychology/a/parenting-style.htm [Accessed 28 Aug. 2013].

Children and Gangs. (n.d.). [online] Available at: https://lsgdotcom.files.wordpress.com/2011/11/qa_research_children_gangs_january2011.pdf [Accessed 7 Jul. 2014].

Children.gov.on.ca, (2010). *Chapter 4: Social Disorganization Theory.* [online] Available at: http://www.children.gov.on.ca/htdocs/English/topics/youthandthelaw/roots/volume5/chapter04_social_disorganization.aspx [Accessed 31 Jan. 2014].

Citizensreportuk.org, (n.d.). *London Teenage Murder 2005 - 2015.* [online] Available at: http://www.citizensreportuk.org/reports/teenage-murder-london.html [Accessed 11 Jun. 2015].

Clark, K. (2006). *Feature Focus: Youth Gangs and Guns.* [online] Available at: http://www.rcmp-grc.gc.ca/yg-ja/gangs-bandes-eng.pdf [Accessed 20 Jun. 2011].

Clark, N. (2013). *The gangs of Britain: New TV series reveals 100 years of organised crime.* [online] Express.co.uk. Available at: http://www.express.co.uk/news/uk/428014/The-gangs-of-Britain-New-TV-series-reveals-100-years-of-organised-crime [Accessed 22 Aug. 2014].

Cliffsnotes.com, (2015). *Theories of Deviance.* [online] Available at: https://www.cliffsnotes.com/study-guides/sociology/deviance-crime-and-social-control/theories-of-deviance [Accessed 1 May 2015].

Clinard, M. (1968). *Sociology of deviant behavior.* New York: Holt, Rinehart and Winston.

Coste, B. (n.d.). *3 Parenting Styles in Depth: The Famous Diana Baumrind Study.* [online] Positive-parenting-ally.com. Available at: http://www.positive-parenting-ally.com/3-parenting-styles.html [Accessed 28 Feb. 2015].

Couldn â€™t Care Less. (2008). [online] Available at: http://www.centreforsocialjustice.org.uk/UserStorage/pdf/Pdf%20reports/Couldn'tCareLess.pdf [Accessed 19 Aug. 2011].

Cowan, R. (2005). *Inquest finds gunman in 15-day siege shot himself.* [online] the Guardian. Available at: http://www.theguardian.com/uk/2005/jan/18/ukcrime.rosiecowan [Accessed 20 Apr. 2009].

Cox, J. (2015). *What causes crime?.* [online] Socialist Worker (Britain). Available at: http://socialistworker.co.uk/art/5494/What+causes+crime%3F [Accessed 19 Jun. 2015].

Cps.gov.uk, (2014). *Dispersal Orders: Legal Guidance:.* [online] Available at: http://www.cps.gov.uk/legal/d_to_g/dispersal_orders/ [Accessed 20 Jan. 2015].

Crimediversionscheme.org.uk, (2011). *HMP Coldingley 1.* [online] Available at: http://www.crimediversionscheme.org.uk/bookaworkshop/hmpcoldingley1.html [Accessed 29 Aug. 2013].

Crimediversionscheme.org.uk, (2011). *HMP Coldingley 3.* [online] Available at: http://www.crimediversionscheme.org.uk/bookaworkshop/hmpcoldingley.html [Accessed 20 Aug. 2012].

Criminology Wiki, (2015). *Social Disorganization Theory.* [online] Available at:

http://criminology.wikia.com/wiki/Social_Disorgani
zation_Theory [Accessed 8 Jul. 2013].

Crossman, (2013). *How Labeling Theory Can Help Us Understand Criminal Behavior.* [online] About.com Education. Available at:
http://sociology.about.com/od/Sociological-
Theory/a/Labeling-Theory.htm [Accessed 25 Aug. 2014].

Crossman, (2013). *Moral Panic.* [online] About.com Education. Available at:
http://sociology.about.com/od/M_Index/g/Moral-
Panic.htm [Accessed 25 Aug. 2014].

Curtis,, P. (2008). *Education: Black Caribbean children held back by institutional racism in schools, says study.* [online] Available at:
http://www.theguardian.com/education/2008/sep/05/
raceineducation.raceinschools [Accessed 27 Sep. 2009].

Doyle, J. (2012). *Under-18s commit a quarter of all crimes: Young offenders responsible for more than a million crimes in just one year.* [online] Mail Online. Available at:
http://www.dailymail.co.uk/news/article-
2150187/Under-18s-commit-quarter-crimes-Young-
offenders-responsible-million-crimes-just-year.html [Accessed 7 Jul. 2013].

Durham, M. and Kellner, D. (2001). *Media and cultural studies.* Malden, Mass.: Blackwell Publishers.

Dying to Belong. (2009). [online] Available at:
http://www.centreforsocialjustice.org.uk/UserStorage
/pdf/Pdf%20reports/DyingtoBelongFullReport.pdf [Accessed 19 Aug. 2011].

Eades, C., Grimshaw, R., Silvestri, A. and Solomon, E. (2007). *â€˜Knife Crimeâ€™ A review of evidence and policy.* [online] Available at:
http://www.crimeandjustice.org.uk/sites/crimeandjus

tice.org.uk/files/ccjs_knife_report.pdf [Accessed 20 Aug. 2013].

Ed.ac.uk, (2013). *Study links school exclusion to prison | News archive |*. [online] Available at: http://www.ed.ac.uk/news/2013/exclusionprison-280213 [Accessed 19 Jan. 2015].

Edwards, J. (2012). *The ten most notorious crime organisations.* [online] mirror. Available at: http://www.mirror.co.uk/news/uk-news/top-ten-criminal-gangs-812916 [Accessed 11 Dec. 2013].

Encyclopedia.com, (2003). *"Gangs." International Encyclopedia of Marriage and Family..* [online] Available at: http://www.encyclopedia.com/doc/1G2-3406900183.html. [Accessed 20 Aug. 2008].

Encyclopedia.com, (2003). *Gangs Facts, information, pictures | Encyclopedia.com articles about Gangs.* [online] Available at: http://www.encyclopedia.com/topic/Gangs.aspx [Accessed 9 Mar. 2014].

eNotes, (2014). *Social Disorganization Theory Research Paper Starter - eNotes.com.* [online] Available at: http://www.enotes.com/research-starters/social-disorganization-theory [Accessed 19 Feb. 2015].

Evening Standard, (2014). *London gang members commit 6600 crimes including 24 murders in three.* [online] Available at: http://www.standard.co.uk/news/crime/london-gang-members-commit-6600-crimes-including-24-murders-in-three-years-9186733.html [Accessed 24 Feb. 2015].

Family.jrank.org, (n.d.). *Gangs - Gangs Internationally.* [online] Available at: http://family.jrank.org/pages/675/Gangs-Gangs-Internationally.html [Accessed 23 Sep. 2009].

Fitch, K. (2009). *Teenagers at risk.* [online] The safeguarding needs of young people in gangs and

violent peer groups. Available at:
http://www.nspcc.org.uk/globalassets/documents/res
earch-reports/teenagers-at-risk-report.pdf [Accessed
18 Feb. 2013].

Foster, J. (1999). *Bulger ruling: If the defendants could
not talk about their crime, how could they conduct a
defence?* [online] The Independent. Available at:
http://www.independent.co.uk/news/uk/crime/bulger
-ruling-if-the-defendants-could-not-talk-about-their-
crime-how-could-they-conduct-a-defence-
739709.html [Accessed 7 May 2011].

Fox, D. and Arnull, E. (2013). *Social Work In The Youth
Justice System.* Maidenhead: McGraw-Hill
Education.

Franko Ass, K. (2007). *Globalization & Crime.* London:
Sag Publication Ltd.

Freelists.org. 2014. [guide.chat] riot 6 street gang called
tottenham mandem - guide.chat - FreeLists. [online]
Available
at:http://www.freelists.org/post/guide.chat/riot-6-
street-gang-called

Gilbertson, D. (n.d.). *Exclusion and Crime Is there a Link
between exclusion from school and Juvenile crime [.*
[online] Available at:
http://www.npi.org.uk/reports/schools%20exclusion.
pdf. [Accessed 12 Aug. 2011].

Goldson, B. and Muncie, J. (2006). *Youth, crime and
justice.* London: SAGE.

Google Books, (2013). *Youth Justice.* [online] Available
at:
https://books.google.co.uk/books?id=ZmhHxxwSW
YIC&pg=PA133&lpg=PA133&dq=deaths+of+youn
g+people+(aged+21+and+under)+in+prisons+and+Y
oung+Offender+Institutions+(YOIs)+by+year+since
+1990.&source=bl&ots=ALBn-
mZhpk&sig=xmH2dNYfsActe3GWKauoVUUj3Lk
&hl=en&sa=X&ved=0CC8Q6AEwAmoVChMIspW

58p7QxwIVJI3bCh0pEw1D [Accessed 23 Aug. 2014].

Gov.uk, (2014). *Narey's report on initial training for children's social workers - Written statements to Parliament - GOV.UK*. [online] Available at: https://www.gov.uk/government/speeches/nareys-report-on-initial-training-for-childrens-social-workers [Accessed 6 Feb. 2015].

Grayling, C. (2009). *TheyWorkForYou*. [online] Theyworkforyou.com. Available at: http://www.theyworkforyou.com/debates/?id=2009-06-09b.657.1 [Accessed 27 Feb. 2011].

Greco, B. (2014). *True Mafia Stories*. Nischal Hegde.

Griggs, J. and Walker, R. (2008). *The costs of child poverty for individuals and society*. [online] Available at: http://www.jrf.org.uk/system/files/2301-child-poverty-costs.pdf [Accessed 19 Aug. 2011].

Grobman, K. (2008). *Diana Baumrind & Parenting Styles*. [online] Devpsy.org. Available at: http://www.devpsy.org/teaching/parent/baumrind_styles.html [Accessed 12 Sep. 2009].

Guardian, (1999). *Yardie terror grips London*. [online] Available at: http://www.theguardian.com/uk/1999/jul/18/ukguns.theobserver [Accessed 7 Jul. 2011].

Hanes, T. (2015). *What Is Verbal Communication? | LIVESTRONG.COM*. [online] LIVESTRONG.COM. Available at: http://www.livestrong.com/article/150573-what-is-verbal-communication/ [Accessed 4 Jul. 2015].

Hanes, T. (2015). *What Is Verbal Communication? | LIVESTRONG.COM*. [online] LIVESTRONG.COM. Available at: http://www.livestrong.com/article/150573-what-is-verbal-communication/ [Accessed 31 Jul. 2015].

Harrison, A. (2014). *Narey's report on initial training for children's social workers - Written statements to Parliament - GOV.UK.* [online] Gov.uk. Available at: https://www.gov.uk/government/speeches/nareys-report-on-initial-training-for-childrens-social-workers [Accessed 19 Aug. 2014].

Herald Scotland, (n.d.). *Our 10 modern evils.* [online] Available at: http://www.heraldscotland.com/news/12767733.Our_10_modern_evils/ [Accessed 27 Feb. 2014].

HM Government, (2013). *Working together to safe guard children.* [online] Available at: https://www.gov.uk/government/uploads/system/uploads/attachment_data/file/417669/Archived-Working_together_to_safeguard_children.pdf [Accessed 18 Aug. 2015].

Howell, J. (1998). *Youth Gangs: An Overview.* [online] Available at: https://secure.ce-credit.com/articles/101181/167249.pdf [Accessed 20 Aug. 2015].

Hutton, R. (2013). *U.K. Gun Curbs Mean More Violence Yet Fewer Deaths Than in U.S..* [online] Bloomberg.com. Available at: http://www.bloomberg.com/news/articles/2013-04-24/u-k-gun-curbs-mean-more-violence-yet-fewer-deaths-than-in-u-s- [Accessed 28 Mar. 2014].

Inquest.org.uk, (2014). *Deaths of children and young people | INQUEST.* [online] Available at: http://www.inquest.org.uk/issues/deaths-of-children-and-young-people [Accessed 18 Jul. 2015].

Interpersonal skills ToolClicks, (n.d.). *Communication skills - Psychological and sociological barriers to communication.* [online] Available at: http://www.cipd.co.uk/toolclicks/interpersonalskills/training-tools/communication-skills/psycho-sociological-boundaries/default.aspx [Accessed 31 Aug. 2014].

Investopedia, (2013). *Conflict Theory Definition | Investopedia*. [online] Available at: http://www.investopedia.com/terms/c/conflict-theory.asp [Accessed 7 Jul. 2014].

Irr.org.uk, (2015). *Criminal justice system statistics | Institute of Race Relations*. [online] Available at: http://www.irr.org.uk/research/statistics/criminal-justice/#_edn2 [Accessed 19 Aug. 2015].

ITV News, (2013). *Chris Grayling announces youth offenders reform*. [online] Available at: http://www.itv.com/news/update/2013-02-14/chris-grayling-announces-youth-offenders-reform/ [Accessed 30 Apr. 2014].

Jones, S. (2010). *Boys, 10 and 11, found guilty of attempted rape of girl, eight*. [online] the Guardian. Available at: http://www.theguardian.com/uk/2010/may/24/boys-found-guilty-attempted-rape [Accessed 5 Aug. 2012].

Jones,, T. (n.d.). *The Kray Twins: Brothers in Arms*. [online] Available at: http://www.trutv.com/library/crime/gangsters_outlaws/mob_bosses/kray/villain_11.html. [Accessed 7 Aug. 2009].

Katz,, I., Corlyon, J., La Placa, V. and Hunter, S. (2007). *The relationship between parenting and poverty*. [online] Available at: http://www.jrf.org.uk/sites/files/jrf/parenting-poverty.pdf [Accessed 28 Aug. 2009].

Labour Left, (2012). *Remembering When Every Child Mattered*. [online] Available at: http://www.labourleft.co.uk/remembering-when-every-child-mattered/ [Accessed 29 Sep. 2014].

Lawmentor.co.uk, (2013). *lawmentor.co.uk - Glossary - Doli incapax*. [online] Available at:

http://www.lawmentor.co.uk/glossary/D/doli-incapax/ [Accessed 6 May 2014].

Lee, E. (2015). *Review and Criticisms of Attachment Theory*. [online] Personalityresearch.org. Available at: http://www.personalityresearch.org/papers/lee.html [Accessed 26 Aug. 2015].

Loc.gov, (2013). *Firearms-Control Legislation and Policy: Great Britain | Law Library of Congress*. [online] Available at: http://www.loc.gov/law/help/firearms-control/greatbritain.php [Accessed 6 Jun. 2014].

Majors, R. (2001). *Educating our Black children*. London: RoutledgeFalmer.

Malins,, H. (2000). *Young Offenders*. [online] Epolitix.com. Available at: http://www.epolitix.com/mpwebsites/mpspeeches/m pspeechdetails/newsarticle/young-offenders///mpsite/humfrey-malins/. [Accessed 12 Mar. 2011].

Malone, A. (2009). *Teen turf wars: Last week a boy known as 'Captain Rocketz' became a victim of gang violence simply because he strayed into the wrong postcode*. [online] Mail Online. Available at: http://www.dailymail.co.uk/news/article-1132757/Teen-turf-wars-Last-week-boy-known-Captain-Rocketz-victim-gang-violence-simply-strayed-wrong-postcode.html [Accessed 23 Aug. 2011].

Marshal, B., Webb, B. and Tilley, N. (2005). *Rationalisation of Current research on guns gangs and other weapons: Phase 1*. [online] Ucl.ac.uk. Available at: http://www.ucl.ac.uk/jdi [Accessed 23 Aug. 2007].

Muller Ph.D., R. (2013). *Poverty, Broken Homes, Violence: The Making of a Gang Member*. [online] Psychology Today. Available at:

https://www.psychologytoday.com/blog/talking-about-trauma/201308/poverty-broken-homes-violence-the-making-gang-member [Accessed 19 Nov. 2014].

Nagra, D. (2010). *Moral Panics: How Media Influences the Legislature.* [online] CJR2010. Available at: https://cjr2010.wordpress.com/2010/06/10/moral-panics-how-media-influences-the-legislature/ [Accessed 19 Aug. 2012].

News Shopper, (2009). *DEPTFORD: Shakilus Townsend 'honey trap' killers jailed.* [online] Available at: http://www.newsshopper.co.uk/news/4580773.DEPT FORD__Shakilus_Townsend__honey_trap__killers_ jailed/ [Accessed 29 Oct. 2010].

News.bbc.co.uk, (2005). *BBC ON THIS DAY | 8 | 1995: Youth gang stabs head teacher to death.* [online] Available at: http://news.bbc.co.uk/onthisday/hi/dates/stories/dece mber/8/newsid_2536000/2536661.stm [Accessed 27 Aug. 2010].

News.bbc.co.uk, (2007). *BBC NEWS | UK | England | London | Police identify 169 London gangs.* [online] Available at: http://news.bbc.co.uk/1/hi/england/london/6383933.s tm [Accessed 19 Aug. 2011].

News.bbc.co.uk, (2007). *BBC NEWS | UK | Magazine | What is a gang?.* [online] Available at: http://news.bbc.co.uk/1/hi/magazine/6683211.stm [Accessed 27 Sep. 2011].

News.bbc.co.uk, (2010). *BBC News - Calls to raise age of criminal responsibility rejected.* [online] Available at: http://news.bbc.co.uk/1/hi/uk/8565619.stm [Accessed 23 Aug. 2012].

News.bbc.co.uk, (2015). *BBC News | UK | Who are the Yardies?.* [online] Available at: http://news.bbc.co.uk/1/hi/uk/371604.stm [Accessed 5 Aug. 2015].

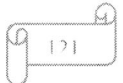

Ojjdp.gov, (2008). *Why Do Youth Join Gangs?*. [online] Available at: http://www.ojjdp.gov/jjbulletin/9808/why.html [Accessed 20 Aug. 2011].

Pall Sveinsson, K. (2012). *Overrepresentation: Continuities and Change.* [online] Criminal Justice v. Racial Justice. Available at: http://www.runnymedetrust.org/uploads/publications /pdfs/CriminalJusticeVRacialJustice-2012.pdf [Accessed 30 Aug. 2014].

Pitts, J. (2008). *Reluctant gangsters.* Cullompton, Devon, UK: Willan Publishing.

Police, M. (2015). *FAQs - Metropolitan Police Service.* [online] Content.met.police.uk. Available at: http://content.met.police.uk/Article/FAQs/14000149 87691/gangcrime [Accessed 20 Aug. 2015].

Police, M. (2015). *History of Trident - Metropolitan Police Service.* [online] Content.met.police.uk. Available at: http://content.met.police.uk/Article/History-of-Trident/1400014986671/gangcrime [Accessed 25 Jun. 2015].

Police, M. (2015). *History of Trident - Metropolitan Police Service.* [online] Content.met.police.uk. Available at: http://content.met.police.uk/Article/History-of-Trident/1400014986671/gangcrime [Accessed 1 May 2015].

Popcenter.org, (2015). *Crime Analysis for Problem Solvers in 60 Small Steps.* [online] Available at: http://www.popcenter.org/learning/60steps/index.cf m?stepNum=8 [Accessed 26 Apr. 2015].

Poverty.ac.uk, (2013). *Impact of austerity on deprived neighbourhoods | Poverty and Social Exclusion.* [online] Available at: http://www.poverty.ac.uk/editorial/impact-austerity-

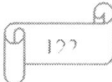

deprived-neighbourhoods [Accessed 7 Aug. 2014].

Puffett, N. (2010). *Government clarifies ban on Every Child Matters.* [online] nql.redesign.cypnow.co.uk. Available at: http://www.cypnow.co.uk/cyp/news/1053008/govern ment-clarifies-ban-every-child-matters [Accessed 18 Aug. 2011].

Research and Media Unit, B. (2011). *Reaching families in need.* [online] Available at: http://www.barnardos.org.uk/reaching_families_in_n eed.pdf [Accessed 18 Aug. 2014].

Richinstyle.com, (2011). *Sentencing.* [online] Available at: http://www.richinstyle.com/masterclass/smallerwhite /sentencing.html [Accessed 19 Jan. 2013].

Richinstyle.com, (2012). *Sentencing.* [online] Available at: http://www.richinstyle.com/masterclass/smallerwhite /sentencing.html [Accessed 20 Aug. 2014].

Roberson, C. and Azaola, E. (2015). *Deviant Behavior.* Boca Raton: CRC Press.

Root, G. (2015). *Attitudinal Barriers to Communication.* [online] Small Business - Chron.com. Available at: http://smallbusiness.chron.com/attitudinal-barriers-communication-11670.html [Accessed 2 Jun. 2015].

Rushing, W. (1968). *Deviant behavior and social process.* Chicago: Rand McNally.

Rutter, M. (1995). Clinical Implications of Attachment Concepts: Retrospect and Prospect. *J Child Psychol & Psychiat*, 36(4), pp.549-571.

Samenow, Ph.D, S. (2011). *Do Prisons Really Make Offenders Worse?.* [online] Psychology Today. Available at: https://www.psychologytoday.com/blog/inside-the-criminal-mind/201104/do-prisons-really-make-offenders-worse [Accessed 13 Sep. 2013].

Schaffer, H. (2004). *Introducing child psychology.* Malden, MA: Blackwell Pub.

Schubert, J. (2013). *Positivist Criminology: Definition & Theory - Video & Lesson Transcript | Study.com.* [online] Study.com. Available at: http://study.com/academy/lesson/positivist-criminology-definition-theory.html [Accessed 26 Aug. 2014].

Siegel, L. (2000). *Criminology.* Belmont, Calif.: Wadsworth/Thomson Learning.

Siegel, L. (2005). *Criminology.* Belmont, CA: Thomson/Wadsworth.

Skillsyouneed.com, (2015). *Verbal Communication Skills | SkillsYouNeed.* [online] Available at: http://www.skillsyouneed.com/ips/verbal-communication.html [Accessed 31 Aug. 2014].

Slack, J. (2009). *Culture of violence: Gun crime goes up by 89% in a decade.* [online] Mail Online. Available at: http://www.dailymail.co.uk/news/article-1223193/Culture-violence-Gun-crime-goes-89-decade.html [Accessed 7 Jul. 2011].

Slay, J. and Penny, J. (2013). *Surviving austerity.* [online] Neweconomics.org. Available at: http://www.neweconomics.org/publications/entry/surviving-austerity [Accessed 5 Nov. 2014].

Smith, M. and Doyle, M. (2013). *Globalization: theory and experience.* [online] infed.org. Available at: http://www.infed.org/biblio/globalization.htm. [Accessed 22 Aug. 2014].

Socialist Worker (Britain), (2002). *London's children: 53% on breadline.* [online] Available at: http://www.socialistworker.co.uk/art.php?id=4272 [Accessed 9 Sep. 2011].

Socialist Worker (Britain), (2007). *Time to take a new direction.* [online] Available at: http://www.socialistworker.co.uk/art.php?id=12917 [Accessed 12 Aug. 2011].

Steele, J. (2007). *Blair: Black community must oppose gangs.* [online] Telegraph.co.uk. Available at: http://www.telegraph.co.uk/news/uknews/1548329/B

lair-Black-community-must-oppose-gangs.html [Accessed 20 Aug. 2011].

Stutz, A. (2006). *Knife Guns and Gangs: Briefing paper from the National Youth Agency.* [online] Available at: http://www.nya.org.uk/shared_asp_files/uploadedfile s/ecd84506-66c4-46c4-885a-4b449fb681c2_spotlight37.pdf. [Accessed 20 Nov. 2008].

Sutherland, A., Brunton-Smith, I. and Jackson, J. (2013). *COLLECTIVE EFFICACY, DEPRIVATION AND VIOLENCE IN LONDON.* [online] Available at: http://www.crim.cam.ac.uk/people/academic_researc h/alex_sutherland/collectiveefficacyinlondon.pdf [Accessed 20 Nov. 2014].

Tackling Gangs. (2008). [online] Available at: http://www.safecolleges.org.uk/sites/default/files/loc al_authorities.pdf [Accessed 9 Sep. 2011].

The Times, (2009). *Guns and Gangs Weapons crime and its deadly link with youth culture must be defeated.* [online] Available at: http://www.timesonline.co.uk/tol/comment/leading_a rticle/article2317305.ece. [Accessed 5 Aug. 2009].

The youth justice system in England and Wales: Reducing offending by young people. (2011). [online] Available at: http://www.publications.parliament.uk/pa/cm201011 /cmselect/cmpubacc/721/721.pdf [Accessed 19 Aug. 2013].

Thompson, K. (1998). *Moral panics.* London: Routledge.

TimeOut, L. (2008). *The Metropolitan Police's Operation Trident on Gun Crime.* [online] TimeOut London. Available at: http://www.timeout.com/london/things-to-do/ten-years-of-operation-trident-2 [Accessed 19 Oct. 2010].

Tititudorancea.net, (2014). *Criminology.* [online] Available at:

https://www.tititudorancea.net/z/criminology.htm
[Accessed 7 Apr. 2015].

Travis, A. (2013). *Young offenders: government plans to put education 'at heart of detention'*. [online] the Guardian. Available at http://www.theguardian.com/society/2013/feb/14/young-offenders-education-detention-academies [Accessed 30 Oct. 2014].

Travis, A. and Khan, S. (2011). *Youth Justice Board saved before expected Lords defeat*. [online] the Guardian. Available at: http://www.theguardian.com/society/2011/nov/23/youth-justice-board-saved [Accessed 19 Oct. 2012].

Travis, A. and Khan, S. (2011). *Youth Justice Board saved before expected Lords defeat*. [online] the Guardian. Available at: http://www.theguardian.com/society/2011/nov/23/youth-justice-board-saved [Accessed 13 Jun. 2013].

Trueman, C. (2014). *Moral Panic - History Learning Site*. [online] History Learning Site. Available at: http://www.historylearningsite.co.uk/sociology/crime-and-deviance/moral-panic/ [Accessed 19 Jan. 2015].

Walker, K. (2012). *I smoked marijuana when I was a teenager, admits rising Labour star*. [online] Mail Online. Available at: http://www.dailymail.co.uk/news/article-2167424/Labour-MP-Chuka-Umunna-I-smoked-marijuana-I-teenager.html [Accessed 20 Sep. 2014].

Wardrop, M. (2010). *Baby P 'failed by incompetent staff from every agency'*. [online] Telegraph.co.uk. Available at: http://www.telegraph.co.uk/news/uknews/baby-p/8086957/Baby-P-failed-by-incompetent-staff-from-every-agency.html [Accessed 13 Sep. 2012].

Webbe, C. (2013). *Operation Trident is effectively over now we are all vulnerable | Claudia Webbe*. [online] the Guardian. Available at:

http://www.theguardian.com/commentisfree/2013/mar/14/operation-trident-effectively-over-murder [Accessed 1 Sep. 2014].

Wellman, A. (2015). *Seven charged after UK's 'largest ever seizure of firearms'.* [online] mirror. Available at: http://www.mirror.co.uk/news/uk-news/seven-charged-after-gun-smuggling-6250924 [Accessed 14 Aug. 2015].

West, D. (1982). *Delinquency, its roots, careers, and prospects.* Cambridge, Mass.: Harvard University Press.

Williams, K. (2004). *Textbook on criminology.* Oxford: Oxford University Press.

Williams, R. (2008). *Rowan Williams: It's adults, not young people, who are a public menace.* [online] the Guardian. Available at: http://www.theguardian.com/commentisfree/2008/feb/26/children [Accessed 12 Sep. 2009].

Wilson, W. (1996). *When work disappears.* New York: Knopf.

Wintour, P. and Dodd, V. (2007). *Blair blames spate of murders on black culture.* [online] the Guardian. Available at: http://www.theguardian.com/politics/2007/apr/12/ukcrime.race [Accessed 5 Mar. 2011].

Womack, S. (2007). *News - Latest breaking UK news.* [online] Telegraph.co.uk. Available at: http://www.telegraph.co.uk/news/main.jhtml?xml=/news/2007/08/10/nbboys110.xml [Accessed 4 Jan. 2011].

Workingtogetheronline.co.uk, (2015). *Introduction.* [online] Available at: http://www.workingtogetheronline.co.uk/chapters/intro.html [Accessed 7 May 2015].

Workingtogetheronline.co.uk, (2015). *Working together to Safeguard Children.* [online] Available at: http://www.workingtogetheronline.co.uk/chapters/intro.html [Accessed 18 Apr. 2015].

Wynne-Jones, J. and Leapman, B. (2008). *Youth gangs triple child murder rate*. [online] Telegraph.co.uk. Available at: http://www.telegraph.co.uk/news/uknews/1576698/Youth-gangs-triple-child-murder-rate.html [Accessed 23 May 2009].

Yahoo Small Business, (n.d.). *Parents in Crisis*. [online] Available at: http://www.geocities.com/Athens/4111/nogangs.html #intro. [Accessed 20 Aug. 2011].

Yearwood, D. and Hayes, R. (2000). *Perceptions of youth crime and youth gangs*. Raleigh, N.C.: N.C. Criminal Justice Analysis Center, Governor's Crime Commission.

Young Black People and the Criminal Justice System. (2007). [online] Available at: http://www.parliament.the-stationery-office.co.uk/pa/cm200607/cmselect/cmhaff/181/181i.pdf [Accessed 19 Aug. 2011].

Youth Crime in England and Wales. (n.d.). [online] Available at: http://www.civitas.org.uk/crime/factsheet-youthoffending.pdf [Accessed 30 Aug. 2014].

Youth Justice Statistics 2012/13. (2014). [online] Available at: https://www.gov.uk/government/uploads/system/uploads/attachment_data/file/278549/youth-justice-stats-2013.pdf [Accessed 19 Aug. 2014].

Youth Justice. (2013). [online] Available at: http://www.publications.parliament.uk/pa/cm201213/cmselect/cmjust/339/339.pdf [Accessed 19 Aug. 2014].

All the lonely people: social isolation and loneliness in County Durham. (2015). [online] Available at: http://www.durham.gov.uk/...lonely...isolation-and-loneliness.[Accessed 1 May 2015].

Lightning Source UK Ltd.
Milton Keynes UK
UKOW02f1053040416

271498UK00001B/2/P